ᴄᴇ ᴉtre

The P.A.R.E.N... Approach

The P.A.R.E.N.T. Approach

How to Teach
Young Moms and Dads
the Art and Skills of Parenting

Jeanne Warren Lindsay, MA

Morning
Glory
Press

Buena Park, California

10-99

ISBN 978-1-932538-85-4 (1-932538-85-2)

The P.A.R.E.N.T. Approach supplements the
seven-book *Teens Parenting* series. Series titles are:
Your Pregnancy and Newborn Journey
Spanish - *Tu embarazo y el nacimiento de tu bebé*
Nurturing Your Newborn
Spanish - *Crianza del recién nacido*
Mommy, I'm Hungry!
Spanish - *¡Mami, tengo hambre!*
Your Baby's First Year
Spanish - *El primer año de tu bebé*
The Challenge of Toddlers
Spanish - *El reto de los párvulos*
Discipline from Birth to Three
Spanish - *La disciplina hasta los tres años*
Teen Dads: Rights, Responsibilities and Joys

Note: The "regular" editions of the above titles are written
at sixth grade reading level.
*Your Pregnancy and Newborn Journey, Nurturing Your Newborn,
Your Baby's First Year,* and *Discipline from Birth to Three*
are also available in easier reading editions
which test GL 2 using the Flesch Grade Level Formula.

MORNING GLORY PRESS, INC.
6595 San Haroldo Way   Buena Park, CA 90620-3748
714/828-1998   1/888-612-8254
email info@morningglorypress.com
www.morningglorypress.com
Printed and bound in the United States of America

Contents

Preface   9

Foreword   11

Introduction   14
 • Teaching to the present • Importance of group
   interaction • Benefits of home visits
 • Curriculum chapter organization
 • Guidelines for teaching teen parents

1   **Prenatal Health — Where Parenting Begins**   22
 • Personalizing the fetus
 • Adoption plan can be responsible parenting
 • Her pregnancy continues • Labor and delivery
 • Session plans, activities • Classroom teaching help
 • Independent study — for credit
 • Not-for-credit teaching — groups
 • Useful for home visits
 • Sample curriculum — ch. 2, *Your Pregnancy and
   Newborn Journey Comprehensive Curriculum Notebook*

**2 Activities for Learning
Reinforce Concepts   48**
• Postpartum HomeStay
• For-credit course description
• Parenting your newborn — suggested minimum
  requirements
• Personalized workbook examples
• Especially for California — and other independent
  study teachers
• Not a school program?
• Parenthood may bring loss
• Parent/baby activities
• Baby, toddler activities
• "My Child" reports
• Activities for parents of toddlers
• Teaching in the classroom • Nutrition activities
• Weekly group session activities
• Discipline activities
• Teaching through home visits
• Sample curriculum — ch. 4, *Your Baby's First Year
  Comprehensive Curriculum Guide*

**3 Reading for Life —
Parent *and* Child**   80
• Making books
• Developing a life-long reading habit
• Teaching concepts through fiction
• For-credit course • How much reading?
• Improving writing skills
• Reading with no school credit?
• Teaching in the classroom
• Not-for-credit groups
• Reading and home visits
• Sample curriculum — ch. 4, *Challenge of Toddlers
  Comprehensive Curriculum Notebook*

**4   Equality in Parenting
     for Dads and Moms**   102
     • Young moms often the focus
     • A father's rights
     • Ten commandments for working with teen dads
     • School and community can help
     • Learning gentle techniques for disciplining
       (teaching) toddler
     • Finding the fathers
     • Rap sessions helpful
     • Special resources for teen dads
     • When baby is crawling
     • Classroom Teaching
     • Group activities
     • Teaching individuals
     • Sample curriculum — ch. 7, *Teen Dads
       Comprehensive Curriculum Notebook*

**5   Nutrition — Good Eating
     for *Two* Generations**   126
     • Starting with pregnancy
     • Fast food reality
     • Portions versus servings
     • Breast is best for baby
     • Breastfeeding at school
     • Teens and breastfeeding in Boulder, CO
     • Introducing solid food
     • Feeding picky toddlers
     • Shopping for food
     • Classroom teaching
     • Not-for-credit group activities
     • Home visit teaching
     • The obesity epidemic
     • Sample curriculum — ch. 4, *Mommy,
       I'm Hungry! Comprehensive Curriculum Notebook*

6 **T**eaching (Disciplining) with

R.E.S.P.E.C.T. 158
Reality — **E**nvironment — **S**elf-esteem —
Patience — **E**nergy — **C**reativity — **T**rust
• **R**espect — the foundation of good discipline
• Discipline is teaching
• Start with students' realities
• Disciplining infants
• **E**nvironment takes planning
• **S**elf-esteem and discipline
• **P**atience required
• **E**nergy for parent and child
• **C**reative approach to discipline
• Ten discipline strategies that work
• **T**rust between parent and child
• Classroom teaching plan
• Not-for-credit group sessions
• Home visit teaching
• Sample curriculum — ch. 6, *Discipline from Birth
to Three Comprehensive Curriculum Notebook*

Appendix 179
Annotated Bibliography 183
Index 189

Preface

"I'm a social worker, and I lead a weekly group with teen parents. Are your resources just for schools or do you have things I could use?"

"I teach parenting through home visits. Would your parenting curriculum work for me?"

"Teen parents at my school meet with me at lunch each Tuesday. They don't earn credit for this activity, but there is no other parenting class for them. How can I best help them be better parents?"

Teachers who use the *Teens Parenting* curriculum say it's a great resource. It works well in the classroom. It is also ideal for independent study teaching, whether as a separate credit course within a comprehensive high school or utilized for students in complete Independent Study programs such as those in California. But will it work in these other situations?

This book is meant to help all those who care about and work with teenage parents. Whether you are a classroom or independent study teacher, a leader of a group of teen parents, or teach teen parents individually through home visits, you will find support, strategies, teaching activities, and other help on these pages.

Each of the six chapters can help you, whatever your teaching situation. Each chapter includes a reprint of curriculum help for a chapter in one of the *Teens Parenting* texts: *Your Pregnancy and Newborn Journey, Your Baby's First Year, The Challenge of Toddlers, Discipline from Birth to Three, Mommy, I'm Hungry!*, and *Teen Dads*. A *Comprehensive Curriculum Notebook* is available for each of these titles. These notebooks contain objectives, teacher help, quizzes, and many activities for each chapter of the books. These reprints are taken from the *Notebooks.*

For the seventh title, *Nurturing Your Newborn,* suggested curriculum is included for independent study during the postpartum homestay. You are welcome to reproduce these activities for use with your students/clients.

See p. 181-182 for a more detailed description of this curriculum including DVDs, board games, and a pregnancy bingo game.

Even if you aren't using the *Teens Parenting* curriculum, however, you will find help here.

If you choose to reproduce and use the activities on these pages, know the pages have been reduced to 60 percent. Enlarge at 150 percent as you copy them for best use with your students/clients.

Jeanne Lindsay   *April, 2008*

Foreword

Raising children ranks among the most important of life's tasks. A parent's decisions, choices and behaviors literally shape another human being's future beginning at the moment of conception and continuing for a lifetime. The growth from two cells through childhood to adulthood is filled with millions of opportunities and possibilities that a mother and father influence. The months of fetal development followed by the years of growth are filled with both potential and vulnerability.

Raising a child is also one of the most challenging of life's tasks. Anyone who has ever raised a child knows how impossible it is to anticipate how a baby changes everything. "It turned my life upside down" is an understatement that only makes sense to someone who has experienced the joys, sorrows, worries, and stresses of being a parent.

Every parent needs information, help, support, suggestions, respite, sleep, strategies, and comfort. That goes in spades for teen parents. Adolescence has been described as a "normally abnormal period of life." The latest research helps us understand why teens act and feel the way they do. It turns out that their brains are under-going some major reconstruction. That's why moodiness, impul-sivity, explosive anger, erratic behavior and withdrawal are all a normal part of the picture. It doesn't take a genius to figure out how adding a pregnancy — probably unplanned — into the mix mul-tiplies the difficulties. The scary statistics for both the teen parent and the child bear witness to the problems each faces.

Even though the prospects would be better if a parent were finished with her or his own teen years, life doesn't always work out that way. Teens do get pregnant. When they do, they need all the help and support they can get for their own sake as well as for the sake of their children. Among other things they need crash courses in fetal development, prenatal health, labor and delivery, child development, child health and nutrition, and parenting skills. And that's just the beginning of the list! Moreover, when teaching all of these topics and others, we must take into consideration the developmental needs of the adolescent her/himself. There are lots of parenting books out there that assume a mature, stable adult is the reader. These books won't be much help to someone with a fif-teen-year-old brain. Because teen parents have special needs, they need special resources. You have such a resource in your hands.

Jeanne Lindsay is one of the nation's best mentors for teen par-ents. Unfortunately there's only one of her. But this book provides the next best thing to having Lindsay as a private coach. It is filled with essential information and guidance to equip you, the reader, to be the most effective mentor possible for the teen parents you have the privilege of helping.

A Cree Indian elder said many years ago, "Children are the purpose of life. We were once children and someone took care of us. Now it is our turn to care." Those who teach, mentor, coach and support teen parents are caring for two children at the same time.

David Walsh, Ph.D.

David Walsh, Ph.D. is an author and speaker on child and teen development and parenting. His best selling book, **Why Do They Act That Way? A Survival Guide to the Adolescent Brain for You and Your Teen,** *explains what happens to the brain on the journey from puberty to adulthood.*

To Jean Brunelli and Sally McCullough
who have helped so many teens, both through their writing
and during their years
at the Tracy High School Infant Center, Cerritos, CA.

Acknowledgments

First, I thank all of the teen parents — students and interviewees — who have taught me so much about life as a very young parent.

I have also learned from the people involved in the two-day trainings I've been doing in my home for several years. These trainings are for teachers and others who work with teen parents, and most of them have chosen to stay at the "Lindsay B&B." (No, I don't operate a real B&B.)

Meredith Adams and Eileen Lader read the manuscript for this book and offered constructive suggestions. I appreciate their help.

Tim Rinker designed the cover and Angela Allen-Hess provided the photos of her students at the Teen Parent Program, Paramount, CA.

Eve Wright again kept the office running and provided lots of proofreading help during this book's development. She is a valuable part of my life.

Helping teen parents become good parents is a wonderful challenge.

Introduction

The P.A.R.E.N.T. Approach — For adolescents, a parent approach to life signifies a huge change. Becoming a parent at 15, even 17 or 18, usually means life as a typical teenager is pretty much over. Young parents still need opportunities to interact with other teens and to have some typical adolescent experiences, but their lives change drastically when they give birth or become dads.

Teens can be good parents. Even some very young teens are able to provide the love and emotional support the baby needs, providing they have family and community support. You are probably involved in providing some of that support or you wouldn't be reading this book.

Helping a young mother or dad become a better parent is one of the most wonderful challenges you can have. Working with an individual who still has one foot in the world of adolescence even as s/he enters the very adult world of parenting means you can improve the lives of two generations.

Statistically, the children of adolescent parents don't do as well as children of adult parents. "Unique Needs of Children Born to Teen Parents," Healthy Teen Network, lists, among other facts:

- Children of teen parents are 50 percent more likely to repeat a grade and are less likely to graduate from high school than children of older parents.
- Children of teen mothers are more likely than those born to older mothers to experience adolescent childbearing, homelessness, juvenile delinquency, and incarceration.
- Though children of teen parents have more health problems than children born to older parents, they receive only half the level of care and treatment.
- Children born to unmarried, high school drop-out teen mothers are ten times more likely to live in poverty than those born to married women over the age of 20.

Your intervention can change these statistics. Whether you are a classroom or independent study teacher, group leader, or home visitor, an important part of your teaching will be developing a personal relationship with your students/clients. Parenting is a very personal thing, and your guidance *will* make a difference.

Teaching to the Present

Developmentally, adolescents simply cannot look very far ahead. They find it difficult to plan their future. When they are pregnant, it may be hard to visualize life with a real baby. When they hold that tiny baby, they may give little thought to caring for a toddler. And parents of toddlers are so engrossed in day-to-day care of their child, they don't want to think much about preschoolers. Teaching to the present stage of their child's development is a big part of effectively teaching adolescent parents.

When you teach through home visits or independent study, focusing on the current stage of the child is possible. If you work with a group, this is a difficult challenge. Do you have pregnant girls along with parents of infants and parents of toddlers? How can you best teach to the present? You want to retain the advantages of group interaction, but how can you still work individually with each client/student?

If you teach a daily class for credit, perhaps you will plan activities for the whole class for part of the time — speakers on topics of interest to everyone, personal growth activities, safety lessons, nutrition discussions, etc. Then part of the time, you might divide your class into at least three groups — prenatal, parents of 0-12-month-old babies, and parents of toddlers. Then plan learning activities which need little supervision for two groups while you discuss relevant topics with the third group.

The Independent Study assignment sheet included in each chapter of each of the *Comprehensive Curriculum Notebooks* provides numerous activities on each topic, activities which don't demand full class participation. As examples, one of these Independent Study assignment sheets is included in each of the following chapters of this book.

It takes a great deal of planning and energy on your part to develop plans suited to the developmental stage of each student's child. When you do, you will make a far greater impact on the development of your students' parenting skills.

If you work with a group once a week, or perhaps even less often, how can you teach to that current stage? The group by definition probably means group activities throughout each session. Probably through discussion you will touch on specific concerns clients have for their babies and toddlers, whatever their ages. Perhaps you can be available for a brief time before or after the group session to respond to individual concerns.

Or could your sessions be staggered? (This might be difficult if participants must rely on public transportation.) If you have two-hour sessions, it might work to have one group come the first 30 minutes, and you would teach specifically to that group. For the next hour, you would lead the entire group, and focus on the second group for the last half hour. Or perhaps another person can help you work with separate groups part of the time.

You can also offer readings that cover the different stages and topics. The *Teens Parenting* series includes books on specific stages: *Your Pregnancy and Newborn Journey* (prenatal);

Nurturing Your Newborn (postpartum); *Your Baby's First Year*,
and *The Challenge of Toddlers* (ages 1-3). The series also
includes books on specific topics: *Mommy, I'm Hungry!* (nutrition, prenatal through preschool); *Discipline from Birth to Three*,
and *Teen Dads* (parenting from Dad's viewpoint, prenatal to age
3). See chapter three for an in-depth discussion of reading as part
of your teaching.

Importance of Group Interaction

A great asset in teaching through home visits or as an independent study teacher is that you can truly teach to your client's
current individual needs. However, group interaction is also an
important part of learning. Can you provide occasional group
sessions for these students?

Independent Study students could meet together at school occasionally. Can you have an occasional group meeting with your
home visit clients? Perhaps you could meet at a park or possibly
even at a student's home.

You might get an outside speaker for some of these meetings.
Other times you would provide activities for the parent and child
to do together such as finger painting, singing, games, etc. An infant center teacher could provide lots of ideas. You would probably always provide food as an added incentive for participants.

The basic California Independent Study program requires
that the student spend one hour with the teacher and complete
20 hours of homework each week. Some California Independent Study teachers have turned this into part-time group work.
In these schools, students come for two or three hours a day,
sometimes for three or four days a week. This adds the important
group interaction component so valuable for young parents.

When I was teaching, I realized that the best part of the
program was the rapport among the students, the family feeling
as some of them expressed it. Teen parents can offer an amazing
amount of help to each other.

Benefits of Home Visits

If you teach through home visits, you know the importance of
the personal approach. If you teach in another setting, is it

possible to visit in your clients' homes occasionally? Some school programs hire the teacher with the understanding that home visits will happen, and provide official time for those visits. Other teachers manage to make time for visits after school. When I was teaching teen parents, I especially liked to make time to visit new referrals to my class. I would tell the potential student about our program, explain that no one was suggesting she must attend the special class, but suggest the various reasons she might like to do so. Did she want to learn more about pregnancy and parenting? Interact with other young women with similar interests? If her boyfriend was there, I would encourage him to join our parenting class, too, if possible.

Sometimes her mother or another adult was present. As I described our program, I occasionally had the feeling that this family had never before had a positive visitor from school. Generally, it seemed, school representatives were complaining about the student's school-related problems. But here was someone who obviously wanted their daughter in this special school program. Parents seemed to appreciate this fact.

When you visit in your client's home, you gain some understanding of the realities of her life. Effective teaching must include an understanding of these realities in students' lives.

Chapter Organization

While the *Teens Parenting* books and *Comprehensive Curriculum Notebooks* are organized by developmental stages and topics, chapters in this book cover broad general aspects of teaching the art and skills of parenting. As *The P.A.R.E.N.T. Approach* suggests through its acronym, these topics include **P**renatal Health — Where Parenting Begins, **A**ctivities for Learning Reinforce Concepts, **R**eading for Life — Parent *and* Child, **E**quality in Parenting for Dads and Moms, **N**utrition — Good Eating for Two Generations, and **T**eaching/Disciplining through **R.E.S.P.E.C.T.** (**R**eality, **E**nvironment, **S**elf-esteem, **P**atience, **E**nergy, **C**reativity, and **T**rust.).

Each chapter contains, in addition to general teaching

suggestions, a reprint of a relevant chapter from one of the
Comprehensive Curriculum Notebooks. Note that the pages here
are reduced to 60 percent of the size in the Notebooks. Enlarge
these copies to 150 percent to fit an 81/2" x 11" sheet of paper.
To do so, you will need to work a bit at flattening out your book
enough to do the reproducing. Using the actual notebooks is easier. See the listing of these
notebooks along with the texts and other resources on pp.
181-182. Each chapter in each notebook contains:

1. Student Objectives
2. Supplementary Resources
3. Teacher Preparation Tips
4. Reading Assignment
5. Learning Activities
6. Enrichment Activities
7. Independent Study Assignment Sheet
8. Chapter Summary
9. Reproducible Activities
10. Quiz (usually for every other chapter)
11. Quiz Key
12. Suggested Responses for Workbook Assignments

Classroom teachers find all of these materials helpful and us-
able. Independent Study teachers (and teachers needing make-up
work for absent students) will concentrate on the activities listed
on the Independent Study assignment sheet. These assignments
are also useful for the divided class which combines teacher-led
activities with student-directed assignments.

Note that some of the activity pages reprinted here contain
references such as "GRADS Competency 2.1.12." This means
this activity can help one teach to a specific proficiency which is
to be taught in the GRADS programs for young parents (in Ohio
and some other states). These proficiencies are probably similar
to your state's Teaching Standards. For more help with tying
the *Teens Parenting* curriculum to a state's required Standards,

please contact Morning Glory Press.

Each of the following chapters will discuss the use of these materials by for-credit teachers. Then attention will be given to those activities especially useful for group leaders, and for home visitors. For example, if your students/clients do not receive school credit for participating in your group, you probably will not use the workbook assignments or quizzes except as discussion guides. Group leaders will find many, perhaps most of the suggested activities useful.

Home visitors will recognize a surprising number of activities suitable for their clients, too.

Guidelines for Teaching Teen Parents

As you teach teen parents the art and skills of parenting:

1. Assume each student is a good person who wants the best for her/his baby.

2. Help young parents believe they are good parents. Other wise, they won't be.

3. Understand and teach that parenting begins at conception.

4. Help students become an expert on their own child — and then recognize they are the experts.

5. Include teen fathers in teaching and services.

6. Include child in assignments as much as possible.

7. Act upon the teachable moments.

8. Choose curriculum designed to meet teen parents' special needs:
   a. Reader friendly
   b. Learning through activities
   c. Lots of interaction between parent/child
   d. Focus on joys of parenting.

9. Believe that teen parents are the best teachers, and act upon that belief.

10. Above all, start with students' realities.

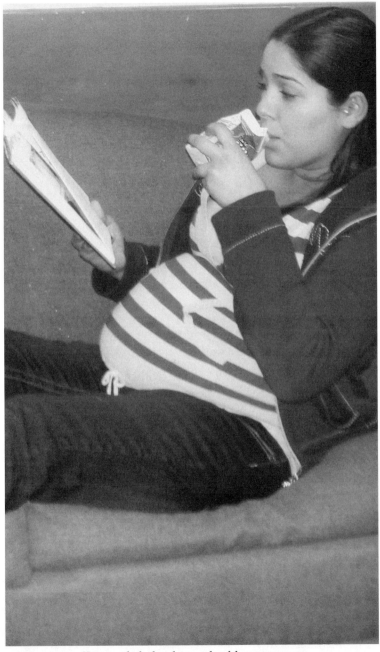

You can help her have a healthy pregnancy.

1

Prenatal Health — Where Parenting Begins

Parenting begins at conception. How she parents during those nine months matters a great deal to her baby, and she probably needs your guidance at least as much now as she will after her baby is born.

As soon as you are aware of a teen's pregnancy, offer your help. Whether this means individual help or an invitation to join your pregnancy/parenting class, independent study program, or pregnant teen group, she needs your assistance.

When she is newly pregnant, she may want most of all to talk about her situation and discuss the decisions she needs to make. Anyone talking with pregnant teens should be aware of her/his own biases. If you can't discuss one or more of the options — adoption, abortion, single parenting, marriage — in an unbiased fashion, you need to be honest and suggest she/they talk with someone who can.

Both young parents need help in dealing with their feelings. Even if the pregnancy was planned (not true for the majority of pregnant teens), the reality may be difficult to accept. Some teens try to ignore the pregnancy for as long as possible. Others attempt to hide it. They may fear the consequences of their family, friends, and/or teachers finding out.

If she confides in you, help her understand the importance of accepting what *is* and moving on. She and her partner need to make the necessary decisions, and change their lifestyle as needed. If she continues her pregnancy, she needs to see a health care provider immediately. Have current referrals available, and it's a good idea to help her keep track of her prenatal health appointments. Help her understand how important these are.

If there is no school program for pregnant teens in your area, it is important to know who in the community can be the teen's health partner. In some areas, there is a perinatal case manager who helps teens with appointments, finding community resources, supports the teen, and links to other programs as needed.

The perinatal case manager generally also does options counseling (termination, adoption, etc.).

Personalizing the Fetus

If she is not considering abortion, encourage her to personalize her fetus. Realizing it is developing into a real baby may help her understand the importance of her lifestyle during pregnancy. What she eats matters a great deal to her baby. Avoiding drugs, alcohol, and cigarettes is an early and very important gift for her child.

A valuable discussion might start with the question, "What does your baby want?" You might suggest she pretend she is her baby. Then ask her to write a letter to her mom (who, of course, is her), and tell Mom what s/he wants her to do so baby will have a healthy life before birth as well as after.

A pregnant woman is likely to be fascinated with fetal development. Understanding her baby's growth through each month may be another reason she decides to take good care of herself. This is a good time for her to keep a journal. Among other things, she can focus on baby's development, perhaps illustrating with drawings of her fetus showing the changes as each month progresses.

An Adoption Plan
Can Be Responsible Parenting

Parents need to make a plan during pregnancy. Will they parent this child themselves? Most pregnant teens plan to parent their child, and they need to plan how they will meet this challenge. Where will they live? How will they support their child financially? Will they be able to continue school? How will their goals change because of their impending parenthood? What new goals will they now have?

Those who consider adoption are also planning for their child's future. In most parts of the country, the birthparents can and should be quite involved in this plan. They may choose the adoptive parents who will rear their child. They may negotiate further contact with those parents and their child.

All of your students need to know about the changes happening in adoption over the past decades. They should know that no longer is it necessary for a birthparent to agree never to see her child again if she places him for adoption. Open adoption is becoming more and more the norm.

Is she going to parent her child because she feels there is no other option? You may want to suggest she make a parenting plan *and* an adoption plan, then choose.

Most pregnant teens are strongly opposed to adoption. However, it is good to know one has choices. To choose parenting when she knows she could release her baby to a family of her choice through open adoption is more freeing than to think she has no choice other than parenting.

For more information on adoption, see *Pregnant? Adoption Is an Option* by Lindsay (Morning Glory Press). The first three chapters are appropriate for pregnant teens generally, and the fourth chapter is about birthfathers. The rest of the book is directed to those interested in thinking about an adoption plan.

Her Pregnancy Continues

During the last month or two of her pregnancy, you'll want to talk to your client about the characteristics and care of a newborn, the importance and techniques of breastfeeding, and how tired she will probably be those first few weeks.

Who will help her with breastfeeding after delivery? If she is only in the hospital one or two days, she needs someone on call after she gets home. As Marina reported when her baby was a week old:

> *Monday I had a breastfeeding doctor's appointment. There were four of us there with our babies, and she had us demonstrate breastfeeding. I thought he was latching on, and it wasn't hurting much, but he was doing it wrong. She had him open his mouth real wide, and then she shoved the nipple way in. It felt totally different. It suddenly didn't hurt at all.*
>
> Marina, 17 - Rudi, 1 week

Having help immediately is likely to make the difference in whether she continues to give her child the gift of breastfeeding or chooses to feed her baby formula.

For more about breastfeeding, see chapter 5, "**N**utrition and Good Eating for Two Generations."

Labor and Delivery

Participating in a childbirth preparation class can help immensely with the labor and delivery process. Have information available concerning such classes, and encourage her to enroll and take her "coach" with her. The coach could be her boyfriend, her mother, father, friend . . . whomever she chooses and is willing. If your teaching involves school credit, can she earn extra credit by participating in a prepared childbirth class?

Can you take your students/clients on a tour of a hospital labor and delivery area? Does she know the best route to take on her "real" trip to the hospital?

Encourage her to make a list of the things she needs to pack to take to the hospital. Even more important, help her make a birth plan. See p. 94 in *Your Pregnancy and Newborn Journey* by Lindsay and Brunelli. After she completes her birth plan, she needs to make a reproducible copy, then prepare enough copies to give one each to her childbirth coach, healthcare provider (doctor, midwife, etc.), admitting nurse, labor/delivery room nurses, doula, and anyone else involved in the birth.

If she plans to breastfeed, this should be included in her birth plan with a highlighted request that her baby be given no bottle in the hospital. The American Academy of Pediatrics highly recommends that all babies be breastfed the first six months, and preferably for a year. You will be helping both mom and baby if you encourage her to make the decision to breastfeed, then help her learn how to do so successfully by knowing who to contact for support at the hospital or in the community.

If a student is considering an adoption plan, suggest she include the role of the potential adoptive parents in her written birth plan. Will they be in the labor and delivery room with her? Will they visit the baby? How much?

One of the most important things for a soon-to-be-parent to understand is the impossibility of spoiling a newborn. If baby is hungry, she needs to be fed immediately. If she's simply lonely, she needs attention.

To help get this point across, have participants in your class or group act out the Reader Theater, "Babies Don't Spoil," reproduced on pp. 29-30. Acting the part of an infant in this skit, then talking about it, will help them understand the needs of their own babies.

Session Plans, Activities

The suggested assignments and activities reproduced for this chapter are planned for chapter 2, "Dealing with Minor Discomforts," *Your Pregnancy and Newborn Journey.* You will find similar assignments and activities for the other chapters in the *Pregnancy and Newborn Journey Comprehensive Curriculum Notebook.* Chapters include "Parenting Starts with Pregnancy," "Your Baby's Development," "Eating Right for Baby and You," "'No' to Smoking, Drugs, Alcohol," "For Some — Adoption Is an Option," "Preparing for Labor and Delivery," "Your Baby Is Born," "The Baby with Special Needs," "Your Fourth Trimester," "Feeding Your Newborn," "What Does a New Baby Do?" "Especially for Dad," and "Another Baby — When?"

The following suggestions for the "Dealing with Minor Discomforts" chapter provide examples of adapting chapter activities to your clients, whether you are a classroom or independent study teacher, group leader, or home visitor. These suggestions can be easily adapted to the other chapters in *Your Pregnancy and Newborn Journey Comprehensive Curriculum Notebook* and text.

On p. 35 you have reprints of objectives, supplementary resources, and teacher preparation tips for "Dealing with Minor Discomforts." Note that a speaker is suggested — a nurse to discuss dealing with minor discomforts of pregnancy, warning signs of problems during pregnancy, and what to do if these warning signs develop.

Occasional speakers provide two advantages. First, you probably don't have expertise in *all* topics, and your students would benefit from hearing other carefully chosen speakers. Second, outside speakers can help your students realize they are important to the community, and, just as important, help the community know about your program. Whether you are teaching a for-credit class or leading weekly group sessions, good speakers are valuable assets.

Classroom Teaching Help

If you teach in a classroom, any/all of the suggestions and activities provided in the *Your Pregnancy and Newborn Journey Comprehensive Curriculum Notebook* will be useful to you. The workbook assignments provide opportunities for the student to react in writing to the concepts found in the chapter. In addition, each workbook chapter includes writing assignments and projects to promote further learning.

You may want to divide your class into two groups, perhaps students in the first two trimesters of pregnancy in one group, and those in the third trimester in the other. You might spend part of your class time teaching the first group about nutrition or the risks of alcohol and drugs while the other group completes workbook assignments over chapters 7-12. The next day, the first group would be assigned to one of the first six chapters in the text and workbook while you discuss labor and delivery or care of the

Your Pregnancy and Newborn Journey, Chapter 12

Babies Don't Spoil

Five babies — Kaelyn, Seamus, Katheryn, Shanita, and Jose — aged one to six weeks, are talking. They're wondering what adults mean when they talk about "spoiling" babies.

Kaelyn: Last night my mom got mad at Grandma. I think it's because Grandma said Mom is spoiling me. What does that mean?

Seamus: Mom said my bottle was spoiled the other day because she left it out of the refrigerator. But what could that have to do with you, Kaelyn?

Katheryn: *(Sadly)* Sometimes they don't feed me when I'm hungry, and I hear that same word. Mom says it isn't time yet. When she says that, she looks at something on her wrist. What does that have to do with me eating? Once when I was crying because I was hungry, I heard them talking. They agreed I'd get spoiled if they fed me when I want to eat. That makes no sense at all. They must think I don't know when I'm hungry.

Shanita: I heard something even more stupid. My aunt Lisa told Mom I *should* cry to exercise my lungs. Exercise my lungs indeed! That's crazy. My lungs are just fine, thank you.

Jose: I think I can explain this spoiling thing. Dad and Mom talked about it this morning — I was eating. Thank goodness they don't tie it in with not feeding me when I'm hungry. Mom's best friend said I'd be spoiled if she picked me up every time I cry. She said if mom does that, I'll expect to be picked up all the time. Then I'd be a spoiled kid. And spoiling evidently is a bad thing. Do you suppose being spoiled means getting picked up when you cry? That's pretty silly, but that's what Mom's friend told her. Why wouldn't they pick me up when I need something? I can't get it myself!

Kaelyn: You know, I think you're right, Jose. Grandma was telling Mom she shouldn't pick me up so often. That's when she said Mom was spoiling me.

Seamus: That's not the same thing as leaving my bottle out to spoil.

Kaelyn: I know. Parents talk funny sometimes. They must mean different things when they say "spoil." But why would she call me spoiled? I still don't know what it means.

Shanita: Dad told Mom he was afraid I'd start whining and crying for nothing if they picked me up every time I cry. Mom told him he was crazy. She asked him how he'd feel if he was in the crib and couldn't get out, he wanted something, and nobody came? She told him if they pick me up when I need something, even if I'm just lonely, I'll probably cry a lot less. He said several people told him not to pick me up too often, but, thank god, he agreed that Mom made more sense.

Katheryn: I think she's right. I try not to, but I know I'm crying more now than I would if they'd feed me when I first get hungry. Mom told Grandma she shouldn't wait more than 20 or 30 minutes to feed me even if the clock said it wasn't time. But 20 to 30 minutes is a *long* time. My stomach hurts a lot when I don't get fed right away.

Seamus: All our parents need to know we don't cry to exercise our lungs, and we don't cry because we're spoiled. We cry because we need something, and we can't do anything about it *except* cry. Maybe if they understood how hard it is for us to wait for food or to be wet or lonely, they'd understand.

Continued on next page

Babies Don't Spoil — p. 2

Katheryn: Maybe we should form a union and stand up for our rights!

All:
We're newborns and we have our rights.
We need your help quite often.
We get you up on many nights
And hope our pain you'll soften.

Refrain:
Long live the rights of newborns
May our cries be answered soon
'Cause if you don't, we get forlorn
And cry a sadder tune.

Remember one thing — You can't spoil us
By picking us up when we cry.
Babies who cry don't do it to fuss
We *need* something, and babies don't lie.

Repeat Refrain
Long live the rights of newborns . . .

So pick us up when we're ready to eat,
Pick us up if we're lonely or sad.
Constantly tell us, "Baby, you're sweet,"
And we'll be the best baby you've had.

Repeat Refrain

Curtain

Discussion Questions

1. Can a newborn be spoiled? Why or why not?

2. If your baby could talk, how do you think s/he would react to such comments as, "Don't pick that baby up so often. You'll spoil her"?

3. How can you tell if it's time to feed your baby?

4. Do you think babies "need to cry to exercise their lungs"? Why or why not?

5. What can a parent do to help her/his child be a fairly contented baby?

newborn with the others.

You would probably discuss chapters 13 and 14 ("Especially for Dads" and "Another Baby? When?") with your entire group. Workbook assignments also provide excellent make-up work for students who are absent.

If you plan to spend a week of daily classes on the topic of minor discomforts during pregnancy, you might plan lessons as follows:

Monday. Start by asking students to write a brief "Dear Dr. Martha" letter (activity #1) describing one or more discomforts they have experienced because of pregnancy. Use these letters as the basis for a class discussion. Then ask students to begin reading the chapter, either singly or, if they prefer, taking turns reading aloud. If you can check out books, perhaps they will finish reading the chapter and complete some of the workbook assignments before tomorrow's class.

Give each student a copy of the Weekly Health Check-Up chart (activity #8, p. 43) and ask her to complete the Sunday part. Then each day this week, spend a couple of minutes checking the previous day's health achievements.

Tuesday. Give each student a 3" x 5" card and ask them to complete activity #4 in which they will describe at least two discomforts of pregnancy together with suggestions for dealing with those discomforts. Suggest they illustrate their cards. Then discuss the information together. Include in the discussion the effect on one's mood of the hormonal changes of pregnancy.

If time permits, ask students to role-play "Moments of Moodiness" (activity #5).

Wednesday. Invite a nurse to discuss dealing with minor discomforts and how to recognize and deal with more serious problems.

Thursday. Give each student the handout, "When do you call the doctor?" (activity #3, p. 41), and talk about how to get emergency help if needed.

Ask students to write an essay in which they discuss the physical and emotional changes experienced during pregnancy (activity #9, and also included in workbook assignments).

Also demonstrate how multiple pillows can add to one's sleeping comfort during pregnancy. Perhaps a student will perform the demonstration.

Friday. Students take the quiz over chapters 1 and 2 (pp. 44-45). When they finish, have supplies available to make and eat a healthy snack.

Or

Have the "Discomforts of Pregnancy" jigsaw puzzle (activity #6, p. 42) available, printed on light cardboard. Ask students to cut the pieces apart, then put them back together. Explain that puzzle pieces within black lines contain a minor discomfort of pregnancy along with suggested remedies.

Or

Have students play the **Pregnancy and Newborn Journey Board Game** and/or **Two-in-One Pregnancy Bingo** (see p. 181). For the board game, choose the blue cards for this topic.

Independent Study — For Credit

If you are an independent study teacher, whether with a formal program (as is often used in California), an independent studies course in a comprehensive high school, or need make-up assignments for an absent student, see p. 38. On this page are the learning activities for this chapter which are deemed appropriate for independent study.

Simply reproduce this page and the assigned learning activities for your student's learning packet. You may choose to delete one or more of the activities if you feel too much work is involved for a specific student. It is quite easy to adjust in this way the work required of a student according to her abilities.

Note: Each chapter in this book (and each chapter in each of the *Comprehensive Curriculum Notebooks*) contains a similarly arranged assignment sheet for Independent Study activities.

Not-for-Credit Teaching

If you are not in the classroom or teaching an independent study student, you probably will not utilize the workbook or quizzes except as discussion guidelines. Or you might decide to use the quiz as a quick pretest to learn more about your students'/ clients' current knowledge and interests.

All of the other assignments would be appropriate for group sessions as well as classroom. If you lead a weekly group, however, you may devote only one or two sessions to an in-depth discussion of minor discomforts of pregnancy, so you'd choose the learning activities you think would most help your clients.

Perhaps at the preceding week's session, you would ask participants to write a "Dear Dr. Martha" letter describing one or more discomforts they have experienced because of pregnancy (activity #1). Use the letters as a basis for discussion. Then you might hand out "When Do You Call the Doctor?" (p. 41) and discuss. Also talk about how to get emergency assistance if needed.

Give each participant a copy of "Dealing with Minor Discomforts" (pp. 39-40), along with a 3" x 5" information card (activity #4). Discussing the information and writing suggestions on the cards for dealing with discomforts they have experienced will reinforce their learning.

Participants might enjoy role-playing "Moments of Moodiness" (activity #5). Discussing reasons for additional moodiness during pregnancy before the role-playing might encourage more dramatic acting.

Role-playing helps students personalize their learning, thus helping them deal with similar situations that arise in their own lives.

Allow a few minutes for participants to complete the Weekly Health Check-Up Chart (activity #8, p. 43). Encourage them to talk about their successes and/or challenges in being good to their unborn child.

Another resource, "Pillows for demonstration of a comfortable sleeping position," is appropriate for group sessions and home visits as well as in the classroom.

Have copies of *Your Pregnancy and Newborn Journey* available for check-out as desired.

In chapter three, we will talk more about the suggested supplementary books.

Useful for Home Visits

If you work with a pregnant teen individually in a non-school setting, usually through home visits, at least half of these learning activities are appropriate. Of the list on pages 36-37, see #3, 4, 6, 7, and 8. First, give her the handout on pp. 39-40, which gives the high points of the text. This is an excellent discussion/teaching guide even if she is not reading the book.

Follow this with the pregnancy discomfort cards (activity #4). Ask what specific discomfort she is experiencing, then suggest she prepare an information card dealing with that discomfort.

Give her the handout, "When Do You Call the Doctor?" (#3, p. 41) and go over it with her. Be sure to discuss how she can get emergency assistance if she needs it.

If you can make the time to prepare the pieces for the "Discomforts of Pregnancy" puzzle (p. 42), she might enjoy putting it together and learn from the experience.

She may have trouble sleeping. Show her how extra pillows (#7) can help. (See illustration on p. 44, *Your Pregnancy and Newborn Journey.*)

Encourage her to keep the weekly health check-up chart (p. 43). Remind her at your next visit that you would like to see it. How is she doing?

The #9 writing assignment provides a basis for an important discussion about the emotional and physical changes she is experiencing during her pregnancy.

Make a copy of *Your Pregnancy and Newborn Journey* available in case she would like to read about the various topics you are discussing with her.

While being part of a peer group is especially valuable for pregnant teens, a home visit can provide the personal approach so important to many pregnant teens. You will know what concerns her the most, and be able to adjust your teaching to her special needs.

Whether you are teaching in the classroom, through group sessions, or in your client's home, know that you are making a positive difference in her life and in her unborn child's life.

Topic: Minor Discomforts
Your Pregnancy and Newborn Journey

Chapter 2

Dealing with Minor Discomforts — pp. 34-47

Objectives: Student will be able to

1. List five minor discomforts often associated with pregnancy together with techniques for dealing with these discomforts.

2. Identify warning signs of problems during pregnancy. (GRADS Competency 2.1.11)

3. Describe how to get emergency assistance if pregnancy complications occur. (GRADS Competency 2.1.12)

SUPPLEMENTARY RESOURCES

Speaker. Nurse discussing dealing with minor discomforts of pregnancy, warning signs of problems during pregnancy, and what to do if these warning signs develop. (GRADS Competency 2.1.12) Also discuss dealing with doctor who always seems rushed.

Pillows for demonstration of comfortable sleeping position.

Supplementary Resource. *Detour for Emmy* by Marilyn Reynolds

Supplementary Resource. *Breaking Free from Partner Abuse* by Mary Marecek

TEACHER PREPARATION—CHAPTER 2

1. **Review Chapter 2,** text, pp. 34-47; the workbook assignments and suggested responses, p. 41 of this *Notebook;* and the quiz over chapters 1 and 2, pp. 38-39. Quiz key is on p. 40.

2. **Review the learning activities,** decide which ones you will use, and reproduce the needed handouts for students. Suggested for this chapter are: "Dealing with Minor Discomforts," pp. 33-34; "When Do You Call the Doctor?" p. 35; "Discomforts of Pregnancy" puzzle, p. 36; "Weekly Health Check-up" chart, p. 37; and the quiz over chapters 1 and 2, pp. 38-39.

3. **Have 3" x 5" cards** ready for Activity #4, and **81/2" x 11" cardboard pieces** for Activity #6.

4. **Schedule the nurse speaker.**

5. **Bring pillows to school** for the sleeping position demonstration.

6. If you decide to use the supplementary resources, obtain copies of *Detour for Emmy* and *Breaking Free from Partner Abuse.* Free one-page study guides are available from Morning Glory Press.

Reprinted with permission
*from **Your Pregnancy and Newborn Journey***
Comprehensive Curriculum Notebook.
Reduced to 60%. To reproduce at full size, enlarge to 150%.

CORE CURRICULUM — GROUP LEARNING

Reading Assignment (individually or together)

Chapter 2, *Your Pregnancy and Newborn Journey,* "Dealing with Minor Discomforts," pp. 34-47.
Discuss. Workbook questions (pp. 6-8) can guide discussion. **Optional:** Students write individual or
group responses to the questions. (Suggested responses to workbook assignments, p. 41, *Notebook*).

LEARNING ACTIVITIES — CHAPTER 2

1. **Discussion Starter.** Ask students to write a "Dear Dr. Martha" letter describing one or more discomforts they have experienced because of pregnancy. Use letters as basis for class discussion.

2. **Speaker.** Nurse discussing dealing with minor discomforts of pregnancy, warning signs of problems during pregnancy, and what to do if these warning signs develop. (GRADS Competency
   2.1.12) Also discuss dealing with doctor who always seems rushed.

3. **Handout.** Give each student a copy of "When Do You Call the Doctor?" p. 35. **Discuss**
   information presented. Also **discuss** how to get emergency assistance if needed.

4. **Pregnancy Discomforts Cards.** Distribute "Dealing with Minor Discomforts," pp. 33-34, to each
   student. Ask each to choose two or more discomforts of pregnancy including the discomforts she
   has experienced. You may choose at least one that is not included in the handout. Prepare a 3" x
   5" **information card** of suggestions for dealing with each discomfort. Suggest students illustrate
   their cards. This project will help reinforce the information students are recording. Tell them to
   keep their information cards handy for reference as needed. After students complete their cards,
   discuss the various suggestions. Have they worked?

5. **Moodiness Role-Play.** Ask students to role-play "Moments of Moodiness." Then discuss the reasons for additional moodiness during pregnancy. Or role-play after your discussion.

6. **Puzzle.** "Discomforts of Pregnancy." Make simple jigsaw puzzles as shown on p. 36, *Notebook.*
   These pieces form seven small puzzles. Each puzzle includes one discomfort (in bold italics) and
   one to four things to do to help one feel better. Copy the page on light cardboard for each student.
   Ask students to cut the pieces apart, shuffle them, and form the seven puzzles. Students may prefer to work in pairs.

7. **Pillow Demonstration** (Adapted from Workbook). Bring pillows (teacher or students) and demonstrate how multiple pillows can add to sleeping comfort in late pregnancy. Encourage students
   to try pillows out in class. As assigned in Workbook, ask each student to try sleeping with a bunch
   of pillows as shown in the illustration on page 44 of the textbook, and then write a paragraph describing her experience.

8. **Weekly Health Check-Up Chart.** Ask students to use chart, p. 37, *Notebook*, to check on their
   prenatal health habits.

Learning activities continued on next page

LEARNING ACTIVITIES — CHAPTER 2 — CONT.

9. **Writing Assignment** (Workbook). How have you felt during pregnancy? Are you sometimes moody and grouchy? Any morning sickness? Backache? If so, what do you do about it? On separate paper, write an essay in which you discuss the physical and emotional changes you're experiencing during your pregnancy.

10. **Quiz.** Chapters 1 and 2, pp. 38-39. **Quiz Key,** p. 40.

ENRICHMENT ACTIVITIES — CHAPTER 2

1. **Write an essay** describing the medical tests commonly done during pregnancy.

2. **Research.** Inquire how to get emergency assistance in your area if pregnancy complications occur. Report your findings.

3. **Supplementary Resource.** Read *Detour for Emmy* by Marilyn Reynolds, a novel about a 15-year-old who has a baby. Complete the one-page study guide. Note: A free one-page study guide is available on request when ordering *Detour for Emmy* from Morning Glory Press. If you prefer more comprehensive assignments over the novel, see the *True-to-Life Series from Hamilton High Fiction Teaching Guide*, also available from Morning Glory Press.

4. **Supplementary Resource.** Suggest that students read *Breaking Free from Partner Abuse* by Marecek (Morning Glory Press). A one-page study guide is free on request from Morning Glory Press. It's a simply written book with the underlying concept that no one deserves to be abused. It offers steps to follow to get out of an abusive situation, but with the full understanding that this may be extremely difficult. The book also includes beautiful poetry on this topic. It is available in Spanish as well as English.

*Reprinted with permission
from Your Pregnancy and Newborn Journey
Comprehensive Curriculum Notebook.
Reduced to 60%. To reproduce at full size, enlarge to 150%.*

Topic: Minor Discomforts
Your Pregnancy and Newborn Journey

Resources:
Text: *Your Pregnancy and Newborn Journey* and Workbook
Handouts:
   "Dealing with Minor Discomforts" p. 33-34.
   "When Do You Call the Doctor?" p. 35.
   "Discomforts of Pregnancy" puzzle, p. 36.
   "Weekly Health Check-up" chart p. 37.
   Quiz over chapters 1 and 2, pp. 38-39.

1. **Read Chapter 2,** *Your Pregnancy and Newborn Journey,* "Dealing with Minor Discomforts," pp. 34-47. Complete assignments in Workbook (pp. 6-8) including writing assignment and project.

2. **Write a "Dear Dr. Martha" letter** describing one or more discomforts you've experienced because of pregnancy.

3. **Handout.** "Dealing with Minor Discomforts" and "When Do You Call the Doctor?" Read, insert in your notebook.

4. **Prepare two or more information cards.** Using 3" x 5" cards, write suggestions for dealing with at least two pregnancy discomforts you've had. Use a separate card for each discomfort. Illustrate your cards. Keep these information cards handy for reference in case you need them.

5. **Activity.** Prepare and work **puzzle,** "Discomforts of Pregnancy."

6. Check your prenatal health habits on your **Weekly Health Check-up Chart.**

7. **Ask your doctor** how to get emergency assistance if you have any pregnancy complications. Report in writing.

8. **Quiz.** Please take the quiz over chapters 1 and 2.

Prepared by Deborah Cashen, author of *Creating Parenting Notebooks*

Your Pregnancy and Newborn Journey — Chapter 2

Dealing with Minor Discomforts

ALWAYS TIRED

✓ Take naps.

✓ Change your position often.

✓ Do activities for which you need to be alert early in the day,
        or right after your nap.

✓ Exercise even when you feel tired. Walking is especially good.

MORNING SICKNESS - Nausea

✓ Drink lukewarm water, eat Jello or popsicles or saltine crackers.

✓ Eat small meals often, or "graze" all day.

✓ Eat something before you go to bed.

✓ Check with your doctor before taking medications to relieve nausea.

✓ Ask your doctor about acupressure wrist bracelets or other non-medicine remedies.

DIZZINESS

✓ Lie down with your feet higher than your head.

✓ Sit down and put your head between your knees.

✓ Breathe as deeply as possible.

✓ Lie down and rest if necessary.

Prepared by Deborah Cashen, author of *Creating Parenting Notebooks*

Your Pregnancy and Newborn Journey — Chapter 2

Dealing with Minor Discomforts (Cont.)

HEARTBURN

✓ Eat frequent, small meals.

✓ Drink liquids (especially water) between meals.

✓ Avoid greasy foods.

✓ Add more fruits and vegetables to your diet.

✓ Avoid lying down right after eating – take a walk instead.

VARICOSE VEINS AND HEMORRHOIDS

✓ Avoid standing for long periods of time.

✓ Elevate your feet higher than your hips several times a day.

✓ Gain 24 – 28 pounds, or up to 40 if you're under 18.

✓ Avoid constipation by *drinking plenty of water.*

✓ Don't smoke.

✓ Exercise the muscles of your lower leg to improve circulation.

✓ Walk throughout the duration of your pregnancy.

BACKACHES

✓ Use heat or ice to relieve (avoid hot tub or Jacuzzi).

✓ Massage back and legs.

✓ Rest with your legs elevated.

✓ Squat (bend from your knees) to pick up things rather than
    bending from your waist.

✓ Stand with your knees relaxed.

Prepared by Deborah Cashen, author of *Creating Parenting Notebooks*

Your Pregnancy and Newborn Journey — Chapter 2

When Do You Call the Doctor?

✓ Problems with vision.

✓ Burning sensation when urinating.

✓ Urination is painful.

✓ You feel you have to urinate but nothing comes out.

✓ Swelling of your face, fingers or lower back.

✓ Headaches that are severe, continuous, or frequent.

✓ Muscular jitteriness or convulsions.

✓ Severe stomach-ache.

✓ Persistent vomiting after your first trimester.

✓ Fluid discharge from vagina (bleeding or amniotic fluid).

✓ Signs of infections (chills, fever, diarrhea).

✓ Change in fetal movement.

Your Pregnancy and Newborn Journey, Chapter 2

Discomforts of Pregnancy

Paste on light cardboard and cut apart for a jigsaw puzzle.
Work the puzzle, then draw a line from each symptom to suggested treatment.

Bladder Infection	See your doctor.	Support your body with several pillows.
Drink liquids.	Eat soda crackers.	**Can't Sleep**
Drink lukewarm water or decaffeinated tea.	**Nausea**	Take medicine only if doctor approves.
Exercise.	Eat frequent small meals.	Put head between knees.
Always tired	Take naps.	**Dizziness**
Heartburn	Eat more fruits and vegetables.	Lie down with feet higher than head.
Eat small meals and avoid greasy foods.	Use a heating pad.	Rest with legs up.
Squat down to pick things up.	**Backache**	Stand with knees relaxed.

Your Pregnancy and Newborn Journey, Chapter 2 (Form developed by Bobbi Ackley)

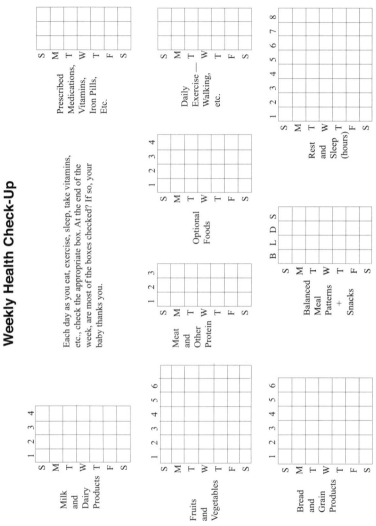

Weekly Health Check-Up

Each day as you eat, exercise, sleep, take vitamins, etc., check the appropriate box. At the end of the week, are most of the boxes checked? If so, your baby thanks you.

Name_____

Your Pregnancy and Newborn Journey
Quiz - Chapters 1 and 2

TRUE/FALSE. Write "T" before the sentence if it is true. Write "F" before it if it is false.

____ 1. It's extremely important that a pregnant teen see a doctor very early in her pregnancy.

____ 2. The baby has a better chance of being healthy if his mother sees a doctor early and regularly throughout her pregnancy.

____ 3. The March of Dimes Birth Defects Foundation can help a pregnant teen find prenatal care resources in her community.

____ 4. A pregnant teen must drop out of school as soon as she "shows."

____ 5. If a pregnant teen is not even in high school yet, she might as well give up and drop out of school.

____ 6. Eating small meals more often may help a young woman cope with morning sickness.

MULTIPLE CHOICE. Circle the letter of all correct answers. Some statements have several correct answers.

7. A pregnant teen
   a. must transfer to a special class for pregnant students.
   b. should drop out of school so she can sleep a lot.
   c. has a right to stay in her regular high school throughout her pregnancy.
   d. may prefer special classes for pregnant students, if available.

8. Most parents of pregnant teens
   a. insist their daughter live in a maternity home during her pregnancy.
   b. throw their daughter out of the house immediately.
   c. are thrilled at the news.
   d. tend to be supportive, although unhappy with the situation.

9. If you feel very tired during your pregnancy
   a. you should stay in bed all day.
   b. it's because your hormones are shifting.
   c. you should exercise anyway.
   d. take naps.

10. If you have a burning sensation when you urinate,
   a. don't worry. It will go away.
   b. you may have a bladder infection.
   c. drinking more liquids may help.
   d. see your doctor.

More quiz items on next page.

Your Pregnancy and Newborn Journey
Quiz - Chapters 1 and 2 — Page 2

11. Why should a mother file for child support if she's not with her baby's father?

12-14. List three ways a pregnant teen's medical expenses may be paid.

  1. _____

  2. _____

  3. _____

15-17. List three things you can do to make you feel better if you have heartburn.

  1. _____

  2. _____

  3. _____

18-21. Check each symptom which, if it happens, means you should call your doctor.
  ___1. Watery, mucousy, or slightly bloody discharge from vagina.
  ___2. Blood from vagina.
  ___3. Sudden increase in discharge from vagina.
  ___4. Decrease or absence of fetal movement.

22-23. Name two places a woman could call for help if her partner abuses her.

  1. _____

  2. _____

24-27. Describe four things that might help if you feel nauseous during pregnancy.

  1. _____

  2. _____

  3. _____

  4. _____

28-33. Write an essay in which you discuss things you can do to feel better during your last few
    weeks of pregnancy. Half of your grade for this essay will depend on the content, and half on
    your writing skills. Use separate paper.

Your Pregnancy and Newborn Journey Quiz Key
Chapters 1 and 2:

1-T

2-T

3-T

4-F

5-F

6-T

7-c, d

8-d

9-b, c, d

10-b, c, d

11-baby needs to be supported by both parents;

12-14: health insurance, Medicaid, some prenatal health clinics are free.

15-17: eat frequent small meals, avoid greasy foods, eat more fruits and vegetables.

18-21: 1, 2, 3, and 4 should be checked.

22-23. Women's shelter, National Coalition Against Domestic Violence.

24-27. Four of the following:
Drink lukewarm water or other liquid.
Eat jello or popsicles.
Eat salty snacks.
Eat small meals more often or "graze" all day.
Try taking vitamins at a different time.
Ask doctor for safe medication.
Ask doctor about an acupressure wrist bracelet.

28-33. Essay on ways to feel better during last few weeks of pregnancy.

Your Pregnancy and Newborn Journey — Chapter Two
Suggested Responses to Workbook Assignments

Dealing with Minor Discomforts
Student Objective:

To list five minor discomforts often associated with pregnancy together with techniques for dealing with these discomforts.

Please read pages 34-47. Answer these questions:

1. Why is a pregnant woman likely to be extra tired during the first three months of pregnancy?
She's extra tired because her hormones shift and her blood supply changes slightly in preparation for the development of the baby.

2. List four things you can do if you feel tired.
*1. Take a nap. 2. Change my position often.
3. Figure out for which activities I need to be alert, and do these things when I'm not so tired.
4. Exercise.*

3. What works for you when you feel extra tired?
Personal response.

4. Do you or did you have morning sickness?
Personal response.

5. List at least four things that might help you feel better when you're nauseous.
*Student should list at least four of the following:
1. Drink lukewarm water or other liquid.
2. Eat jello or popsicles. 3. Eat salty snacks.
4. Eat small meals more often — or "graze" all day.
5. Try taking my vitamins at a different time.
6. Ask my doctor if there is a safe medication I could try. 7. Ask doctor about an acupressure wrist bracelet.*

6. Describe three symptoms which could mean you have a bladder infection.
1. Burning sensation when I urinate. 2. A feeling I have to urinate but little comes out. 3. Urinating is painful.

7. If you think you have a bladder infection, what can you do that might help you feel better?
Drinking liquids often helps.

8. Do you ever feel dizzy? *Personal response.*
Describe two things you could do if you feel dizzy.
*1. Lie down with my feet higher than my head.
2. Put my head between my knees and breathe as deeply as possible.*

9. Are you more moody or crabby than usual now that you're pregnant? *Personal response.*
Why is a pregnant woman sometimes moody?
Hormones in her body are changing. She may have lots of things on her mind.

10. List five things you can do to prevent heartburn.
1. Eat small meals often. 2. Drink fluids between meals. 3. Avoid greasy foods. 4. Eat more fruits and vegetables. 5. Avoid lying down right after eating.

11. How can you avoid constipation? Describe three things you can do.
1. Eat lots of fiber-rich foods. 2. Drink lots of water, juices, and milk. 3. Exercise each day.

12. List five things you can do to prevent varicose veins and hemorrhoids.
*Response should include five of the following:
1. Avoid standing or sitting for long periods.
2. Elevate my feet higher than my hips. 3. Don't gain too much weight. 4. Avoid constipation. 5. Don't smoke. 6. Exercise the calf muscles — walking is good.*

13. Why is it better not to sleep on your back toward the end of pregnancy?
When I'm on my back I might squeeze the large blood vessel which could reduce the blood supply to the baby and me.

14. Describe five things you can do to avoid backache. Check those things you've tried.
*1. Use heat on my back.
2. Have someone massage my back.
3. Rest with my legs up.
4. Squat down to pick things up from the floor.
5. Stand with my knees relaxed.*

15. How do you do a "kick count"?
Lie on my side and count how long it takes baby to move ten times.

Why might your doctor tell you to do this between your 28th and 30th weeks of pregnancy?
Kick counts can reassure you that the baby is okay.

16. Describe ten things which, if any of them happen to you, means you should call your doctor.
1. Problems with vision. 2. Swelling of face, fingers, or lower back. 3. Headaches. 4. Muscular jitteriness or convulsions. 5. Severe stomach-ache. 6. Persistent vomiting. 7. Fluid discharge from vagina. 8. Signs of infections — chills, fever, burning during urination, diarrhea 9. Pain in abdomen 10. Change in fetal movements.

Writing Assignment:

How have you felt during pregnancy? Are you sometimes moody and grouchy? Any morning sickness? Backache? If so, what do you do about it? On separate paper, write an essay in which you discuss the physical and emotional changes you're experiencing during your pregnancy.

Project:

Try sleeping with a bunch of pillows as shown in the illustration on page 44. Then write a paragraph describing your experience.

Take the quiz over chapters 1 and 2.

*Reprinted with permission
from **Your Pregnancy and Newborn Journey
Comprehensive Curriculum Notebook.**
Reduced to 60%. To reproduce at full size, enlarge to 150%.*

They're learning labor and delivery terms
as they play pregnancy bingo.

2

Activities for Learning Reinforce Concepts

P.A.R.E.N.T. — **A** is for **A**ctivities, learning activities. Many people learn best through doing. Reading is a great learning tool, but it doesn't work well for everyone. And those of us who like to read, and perhaps learn best through the written word, appreciate activities along with the reading.

Actually, we know through recent brain research that most people learn best through doing. Including a variety of activities in your plans is likely to help your students learn more effectively.

The last chapter offered activities to help your students learn about the discomforts of pregnancy.

Activities relevant to teaching parenting are often easier to develop when your students have babies or toddlers. They are actively learning as they parent. The new concepts you teach can be reinforced beautifully with activities, especially if those activities involve their child/children. So assign parent/child activities frequently, and allow time for discussion of results.

Postpartum HomeStay

Even if you're teaching a school program, your students will probably be absent two to six weeks after childbirth. Six weeks postpartum HomeStay is almost always better for Mom and baby than rushing back to school as soon as she possibly can after delivery.

Six weeks gives parent and child time to bond, and if she's breastfeeding, to get a good start.

If you lead a group, she may miss only a session or two, and if you're a home visitor, your visits are more important than ever during this fourth trimester.

Learning activities will happen as she/they live with their newborn. The challenge for school credit programs is to help make it possible for her to earn credit while she's home with her baby.

What does a young mother need most during those first weeks after the birth of her baby?

1. Bonding with baby is most important for her and for baby.
2. She needs to establish a feeding routine, preferably breast-feeding. To do this, she needs the support of those around her, and someone to guide her as needed.
3. She needs to take care of herself. Rest is important.
4. If she's in school, she needs to earn credit. (Notice that, important as this is, it is at the bottom of this list.)

At the same time, what does the school need from the student? Too often, the goal seems to be to get her back in the classroom, full time, as quickly as possible, although both she and her baby would be better off spending the first 4-6 weeks getting acquainted with each other. So what the school really needs:

1. Most important, the school needs to meet the student's needs.
2. If this can include generating funding for her school involvement, both win.

Note: If you either lead a group or teach through home visits, and academic credit is not involved, the following outline of the credit course provides a good discussion guide.

For-Credit Course Description

In schools across the country, teachers go to great lengths to develop infant care programs and preschool sessions in which high school students develop care giving skills. Your students will learn about parenting and infant care as they care for their newborns at home, probably far more than they learn in a semester of working in a childcare center.

A young mom is likely to be out of school for several weeks after childbirth, and during this time she will spend many hours each day caring for and bonding with her child. For this she deserves to be earning elective credit just as she would if she were working in a day care center at school.

To be academically defensible in many school districts, however, this parenting credit must be backed up with some documentation. To earn the credit, you can ask her to complete the six requirements as described below under "Suggested Minimum Requirements."

Parenting Your Newborn —
Suggested Minimum Requirements

Reprinted from Student (Independent Study) Workbook
*for **Nurturing Your Newborn***

1. Student will take major responsibility for care of her child from birth to one month of age.

2. Student will record one day each week for two weeks the time she spends with her child and in performing other tasks involved in caring for her baby — formula preparation, laundry, etc. Include cuddling time!

3. Student will read *Nurturing Your Newborn: Young Parents' Guide to Baby's First Month*. She will complete the writing assignments and projects for each chapter in the workbook, as directed by the teacher. She will also take the quizzes over the book.

4. Student will keep a journal in which she writes at least once daily, five days per week, for at least three weeks. In her journal, she is to concentrate on writing about her baby

and her relationship with him/her.

5. Student will keep a record of the money she spends for her baby. For one month, she is to keep track of everything she or anyone else buys for the baby. She should keep an accurate record of the cost of formula she buys, the clothes, diapers, toys, furniture, etc. If possible, include cost of items already purchased when her baby was born. Her expense record should include the total spent for baby by the time s/he is one month old.

6. Student will discuss her progress with her teacher or other person as directed.

Note that keeping a daily journal and two 24-hour time-with-baby records are required in addition to the writing assignments. Explain that the most important, hardest, and most time-consuming part of this course is caring for the new baby. The student receives credit for this parenting achievement, but must document at least part of the time she spends doing so.

Your student will need a copy of *Nurturing Your Newborn: Young Parents' Guide to Baby's First Month* (Lindsay and Brunelli) and the separate workbook. Please check the workbook. Do you need to individualize the assignments for your students? Is there perhaps more writing than you can expect one student to do during her incredibly busy first month with baby? Or do you need to add additional supplementary and enriching assignments?

Each chapter in the workbook contains writing assignment(s), project(s), and a parent/baby assignment.

Note: A personalized version of the *Nurturing Your Newborn* Workbook is available on disk from Morning Glory Press. Baby's name can replace "your baby" throughout the workbook with one computer "change" on the document. See pp. 53-54 for sample pages.

Ideally, you will be able to discuss these requirements with your student before she delivers. You might encourage her to take *Nurturing Your Newborn* to the hospital in case she finds she'd like to read about her little newborn while she's there.

Perhaps your new mom students come to school for brief

Chapter Four
Joshua's Goal — To Be Comfortable

As you read this chapter you'll learn about techniques for helping Joshua feel comfortable, and of the impossibility of "spoiling" him by picking him up when he cries. You'll also read about bathing Joshua.

Please read pages 46-55 and answer these questions:

1. What is most important to newborn Joshua?

2. Does it make sense to let Joshua "cry it out" rather than picking him up and comforting him when he's crying? Why or why not?

3. Describe a good way to pick up Joshua.

4. What can you do to help Joshua's brain develop as well as possible?

5. According to research, which baby is more likely to cry when he's a year old — the baby who was picked up often as an infant or the baby who was left to cry so he "wouldn't be spoiled"?

6. If Joshua cries after being fed, what does he probably need?

7. List at least five reasons an infant may cry.
   1.   2.   3.
   4.   5.

8. How should you bathe Joshua until his umbilical cord has fallen off?

9. Describe Joshua's first bath.

10. Why should you test Joshua's bath water with your elbow?

Reprinted with permission from *Nurturing Your Newborn*
Personalized Workbook Disk (Boys)
To reproduce for students/clients, enlarge to 150%.

11. Should you use cotton-tipped sticks to clean Rachel's nose, ears, or navel? _____.

12. Are you using disposable diapers, cloth diapers you wash yourself, or a diaper service? Why did you make this choice?

13. What is swaddling?

  Try swaddling Rachel. How did she react?

Writing Assignments:

1. Pretend you are Rachel. Why do you cry? What do you want from your parents? How do you feel when no one answers your cries? Write a paragraph describing your feelings.

2. Write an essay in which you describe *your* feelings and how you react when Rachel cries. Be creative in your writing and use lots of descriptive adjectives.

Project:

  Collect ideas from at least five other parents for dealing with a crying baby. Make a list of their suggestions.

  1.
  2.
  3.
  4.
  5.

Activity:

Complete the acrostic activity, "Infant Crying Patterns," page 15.

Parent/Baby Assignment:

Choose a time when Rachel is tired and fussy. Try several methods of soothing him. Describe your efforts in your journal.

periods soon after delivery. If so, or if you can show videos in their homes, we recommend Baby's First Year Series, Volume 1, "Nurturing Your Newborn" (Morning Glory Press). Another excellent video series is "Teen Breastfeeding: The Natural Choice" and "Teen Breastfeeding: Starting Out Right." See bibliography.

Please note: The student's interaction with her child is most important throughout this first month. You don't want to add additional stress to her life. However, she probably wants and needs support, encouragement and even advice during these weeks. If you and she can find a way for her to bond with her baby, learn about parenting her newborn, and earn credit, everybody wins!

Especially for California — and Other Independent Study Teachers

In California some students enroll in the short-term Independent Study program during their postpartum HomeStay. State guidelines require that these students spend 15-20 hours on homework assignments each week that credit is granted. Particularly difficult for new moms is the rule that these hours must be spent each week. The hours of study cannot be "banked," i.e., "makeup" or even working ahead is not part of the program.

The good news is that the independent study concept is easily interpreted to encourage learning throughout the early parenting time, learning which results in earning school credit. Wherever you live, this is a good goal for your students, as long as you and your student understand that bonding with the new baby has top priority during this time.

All new parents learn a great deal that first month. If that learning is somewhat structured and includes communication with a caring teacher, it can be a win-win situation.

Nurturing Your Newborn is a 96-page book covering only the truly important concepts young parents need to learn during that all-important first month. With a copy of the book and the workbook, plus occasional teacher/student contact, the young parent can gain valuable understanding of her new parenting role.

If you're in a district where actual hours of work are counted as school credit, include baby-care as part of those hours. She's learning more in her real-life baby-care laboratory than she would in several months working an hour a day in a school's infant center.

Journal writing is an important part of this course. Suggest that your student keep her journal to share with her child ten or fifteen years from now.

Because the Workbook is carefully planned especially for the student's postpartum HomeStay, no separate lesson plan is needed.

In the California Independent Study program, students sometimes concentrate on only two or three courses at a time. The material described here could be easily expanded into two full-credit, academically defensible courses. One, probably an elective, can be titled Parenting Your Newborn (Child Development, if your district prefers), while the second is designed for language arts credit. The journal and all the writing assignments fit easily into a language arts course.

To complete the language arts course, assign a couple of novels. Good choices are *Detour for Emmy* (story of 15-year-old who has a baby) and *Baby Help* (young father physically abuses baby's mom), both by Marilyn Reynolds (Morning Glory Press). Both novels fit the theme of the two courses. A teacher's guide is available for each novel, guides which contain many activities that fit into standards-based learning.

Not a School Program?

The postpartum HomeStay is a time when you may be glad your client is not taking this course for credit. Completing the assignments in the workbook take time she might prefer to spend with her baby. Knowing her efforts will not be graded may make her interaction with her baby a little more free and natural.

Some of the activities in the curriculum work well with one-on-one intereaction in your home visits.

Just as you might do in the classroom, encourage clients, even if they're not working for credit, to keep a journal during this important time. Suggest they write with the idea of sharing their observations with their child 15 years from now.

As you know, the postpartum homestay is an extremely important part of a mother's life. Your help at this time increases the chance that this transition to parenthood goes smoothly.

Parenthood May Bring Loss

Two to three percent of pregnant teens make and carry out an adoption plan, about one/third abort, and 14 percent miscarry. In any of these situations, she will have to deal with loss.

If she parents, loss is still there. She is losing her adolescence, and she may experience a feeling of loss of self. You need to help her deal with these losses.

Of course your job is to help your clients/students develop problem-solving skills. You don't tell them what to do or try to solve their problems for them. Instead, you need to coach, guide, provide resources, tools and experiences.

Know that you will make a great difference in the lives you touch — whether through classroom or independent study teaching, as a group leader, or as a home visitor.

Parent/Baby Activities

In *Your Baby's First Year,* three chapters, one for each four-month period of the child's first year, focus on playing with and enjoying one's child as well as providing good physical care. The tie between play and brain development is discussed. Included are directions for making toys suitable for the child at various stages, with the understanding the parent will use the toy to play with the child..

Lots of loving interaction with their children is an important part of parenting. A busy adolescent parent sometimes finds this hard to do. Simply taking physical care of their child is difficult.

Help them find the joys in parenting. Assign parent/child activities frequently. If they make a toy in class, the important part of their assignment, as mentioned above, is to play with the toy with the child.

Examples of Learning Activities
from *The Challenge of Toddlers*
Comprehensive Curriculum Notebook (CCN)

1. **Parent/Child Assignment** (Workbook). Play the labeling game (pp. 23-24, text) with your child. Report results in your journal. (Chapter 1)
2. **Role-Play.** Divide class into small groups. Ask several groups to role-play an incident in which a toddler has a tantrum — and to follow with another role-play in which the parent/caregiver either prevents or lessens the severity of the tantrum (i.e., giving child choices). Ask the other groups to role-play the steps which should be followed when a child asks for help. See list on page 36 of the text. (Chapter 2)
3. **Crossword Puzzle.** "Playing with Your Toddler," p. 44, *CCN*. Suggest that students work in pairs to complete the crossword puzzle, then discuss concepts embedded in puzzle. (Chapter 3)
4. **Reader Theater.** "Meghan and Tim Bathe Angel," p. 59, *CCN*. Use as a starter for discussion on father's involvement in parenting. (Chapter 5)
5. **Make posters** on child nutrition. (Chapter 6)
6. **Book Project** (Workbook). Each student can make a book for her/his child. The cardboard from panty hose packages works well. Poke holes along the side and tie with bright yarn. Tell students to write a story about their child — perhaps describe a day in his life. Illustrate it with photographs of parent and child, with their own drawings, or with pictures cut out of magazines. Tell them to read their story to their child. (Chapter 8)
7. **Demonstration.** Borrow two or three toddlers for a class session. Ask two sets of two students to bring ingredients and make finger-paint as suggested on p. 128 of the text and p. 92, *CCN*. Then let the guest toddlers finger-paint — and/or simply let students finger-paint to encourage them to guide their children into this art activity. (Chapter 9)
8. **Prepare basic first aid kits.** Perhaps funding for the materials could be obtained from your local Red Cross, Lions Club, or other service organization. (GRADS Competency 6.4.3) (Chapter 10)
9. **Posters/Bulletin Board.** Ask students to create posters and/or a bulletin board display illustrating possible problems in early marriage together with possible solutions to those problems. (Chapter 12)
10. **Art Project.** Create collages depicting the effect of parents' gang involvement on their children. (Chapter 13)
11. **Newsletter or Booklet.** Assign class members, individually or in groups, to research specific helping resources in the community. After they have gotten the information, they are to write an article about the kind of help offered together with addresses and phone numbers. Compile the results into a Community Resources newsletter or booklet. (Chapter 14)
12. **Play Challenge of Toddlers board game** to reinforce text. See p. 182.

take a few notes may make them more observant.

Tell a young father you would like him to report on the games he plays with his daughter, the pictures they look at together, her food likes and dislikes, her sleeping habits, and other daily activities. Ask the father to discuss his discipline strategies and his feelings about his child at this point.

You may have students who insist they "don't give oral reports." Explain that this is their chance to talk about their own babies for at least ten minutes without interruption. If a student is quite reluctant, ask her to report on one specific activity. If her son is eight months old, suggest she give him a container full of small, safe items from the kitchen. Tell her to watch him for 20 minutes, then share with the class his reactions to the play materials. She may find giving an oral report is not as big a problem as she expected.

Students' oral reports on their child's developmental stage is a wonderful way to teach developmental stages to the other students.

Teaching in the Classroom

Reproduced on pp. 66-79 are the lesson plans for Chapter 4, "Health Care for Your Baby," *Your Baby's First Year Comprehensive Curriculum Notebook*. Asking students to read the chapter and complete the workbook assignments provides good background for class discussions and activities. Will you assign the reading and workbook as homework? Or allow time in class for reading? Or will you and the students read the chapter aloud?

Lesson plans for a week's study of this topic could be:

Monday. Whether they've read the material or not, discuss the chapter summary, "Health Care for Your Baby" (activity #1, p. 69). Ask those who have had a sick baby or a baby with colic to discuss their experiences and share their strategies for making baby more comfortable (activity #2).

Tuesday. Ask two students to read dramatically, "How Can I Help You, Baby?" (activity #5, p. 73-74). Encourage them to rehearse before performing for the class.

Examples of Learning Activities
from *Mommy, I'm Hungry!*
Comprehensive Curriculum Notebook (CCN)

1. **Poster.** Create a poster illustrating portions versus servings of food. (Chapter 1)
2. **Class Project.** Have class plan a party for pregnant teens and breastfeeding mothers and their babies. What healthy snacks will they serve? Plan food totaling about 1000 calories, 25-30 grams of protein, 90-100 grams of carbohydrate, and no more than 40 grams of fat per person. (Chapter 2)
3. **Food Preparation Project.** (Workbook) Prepare three kinds of food for a 7-month-old baby — a fruit, vegetable, and something he can eat with his fingers. Find a 7-month-old baby and feed these foods to him. How does he react? (Chapter 3)
4. **Food Plans for Picky Toddlers puzzle,** p. 97, *CCN*. Students may prefer to work the puzzle in pairs. (Chapter 5)
5. **Class Project.** Invite several preschoolers to class and serve them healthy snacks prepared ahead of time by your students. (Chapter 6)
6. **Parent/Child Assignment.** Exercise actively with your child for 30 minutes. (Chapter 7)
7. **Parent/Child Activity.** Prepare a nutritious vegetarian lunch for you and your child. (Chapter 8)
8. **Field Trip** (Workbook). Visit a child care center. Ask about the food served to the children. What nutrition guidelines do they follow? Do they cater (or not cater) to each child's preferred way of eating? Ask for a few lunch menus, then analyze nutritional content of the meals. (Chapter 9)
9. **Child Care Food Project.** Divide students into small groups. Each group is to imagine they are offering child care in their homes. Assume five children come each day, aged 1-5 years. Ask each group to develop menus for breakfast, snacks, and lunch for the children for five days. They need to serve food that will supply at least 3/4 of the nutrients needed for each child for the day. They will need to make some adaptations to make the food suitable for the one-year-old as well as the older children. They also need to consider the cost in dollars and preparation time. (Chapter 9)
10. **Supermarket/Convenience Store Comparison.** Can most of the students get to a supermarket and to a convenience store, or perhaps a mom and pop store? Give them a list of commonly bought foods, and ask them to compare prices. The list might include in-season fruit (winter - oranges, summer - peaches, for example), 10 pounds of flour, 5 pounds of brown rice, oatmeal, etc. See sample list on p. 170, *CCN*. (Chapter 10)
11. **Recipe Serving Changes.** Talk about changing recipe size to fit one's family. For a four-serving recipe, they halve it for two people, double it for eight, etc. Ask them to do this exercise for the recipes on the form, p. 184, *CCN*. Answer key is on p. 192, *CCN*. (Chapter 11)

Another dramatic presentation would be a student reading Marlene's journal (activity #6, p. 72) as a monologue. She will need a doll as a prop — unless she has her own baby with her. Follow by asking each student to write a note to Marlene, trying to cheer her up during this difficult week (activity #7).

Wednesday. Invite a medical person to talk with participants about immunization schedules, health tips for babies, etc. (activity #3).

Thursday. Discuss the handout, "When Do You Call the Doctor?" (activity #12, p. 70), then ask students to write a detailed report of a time when their baby was sick (activity #11, also a workbook assignment). If the baby hasn't been sick, tell her to interview another parent who has had this experience, and write a report of the interview.

Also discuss determining when to seek emergency care.

Each parent needs to be keeping a health record for her baby. If necessary, use class time to prepare these records. See activity #10.

As homework, assign parent/child activity #13. Choose a time when baby is tired and fussy, perhaps not feeling well. Try several methods of soothing her, and describe efforts in your journal. Also discuss in class the following day.

Friday. Show the DVD, "Keeping Baby Healthy" (activity #4), and discuss. See DVD discussion guide, p. 75.

Follow this with the quiz (activity #14, p. 76) over this chapter.

If time permits, students can work the "Illness and Prevention" crossword puzzle (activity #9, p. 71) individually or in pairs. Discuss the concepts illustrated in the puzzle.

For extra credit, suggest the enrichment activity — writing a skit about baby's first visit to the healthcare provider.

Weekly Group Session Activities

Almost all of the above activities are also suitable for not-for-credit groups. Make the book available to those who want to

Examples of Learning Activities from the *Discipline from Birth to Three Comprehensive Curriculum Notebook (CCN)*

1. **Parent/Child Assignment.** Develop rules for your child, rules appropriate at his/her current age. (If your child is still an infant, the "rules" will be for you.) List your rules in your journal. (Chapter 1)

2. **PSAs.** Ask students, working in groups, to create public service announcements or posters stressing dangers in shaking infant. (Chapter 2)

3. **Project.** Encourage students to make a pullover bib for their child. Suggest that putting an easily washed bib on baby when he feeds himself can make it easier for Mom and Dad to remember that being messy is part of learning to feed oneself. (Chapter 3)

4. **Homework** (Workbook). Crawl through your house at your child's eye level. What do you see that would be inviting to a child? What needs to be done to make your house safe for your child and your possessions safe from your child? Write a report of your survey. (Chapter 4)

5. **Reader Theater.** "Mark Bit Jessica!" pp. 75-76, *CCN*. Four students practice reading the parts, then present the play to the class. Use it to start a discussion about biting, reasons for, how to deal with it, etc. (Chapter 5)

6. **Project** (adapted from Workbook). Ask each student to find a two-year-old to study and follow her around for two hours. Did she ever get frustrated or do things student didn't want her to do? If so, what do they think triggered the misbehavior? Ask them to share results in class. (Chapter 7)

7. **Role-Play.** Ask several pairs of students to role-play a parent and child (aged 2-3 years) shopping in a supermarket. The toddler is causing lots of stress for the parent. Discuss possible solutions to problems. (Chapter 8)

8. **Art Project.** Ask students to create collages depicting the effect of violence on children. (Chapter 10)

9. **Plan a week of activities** for two mothers, each with two children, a 10-month-old and a 2 1/2-year-old. They each will take a two-hour break each week. To do so, each will have "school" for their four children once a week while the other has her time off. Plan two weeks of activities (four sessions with all four children). (Chapter 11)

10. **Role-Play.** Divide class into small groups. Ask each to write a short skit illustrating parents disagreeing over disciplining their toddler. Allow time for each group to act out their play for the rest of the class. (Chapter 12)

11. **Class Project.** Compile a list of places parents can get help. Include hotlines and other counseling services. Check phone numbers and addresses for accuracy. Prepare directory; distribute to students. (Chapter 13)

12. **Brainstorm.** First, brainstorm problems likely to be encountered if child lives with lots of other people. List problems on board. Then brainstorm possible solutions to those problems. (Chapter 14)

13. **Play the Discipline from Birth to Three board game**. See p. 181.

read it, but you probably would not use the workbook except as a discussion guide. The speaker, DVD (guide, p. 75), Reader's Theater (pp. 73-74), and dramatic monologue (p. 72) all fit into the group format.

They, too, need to be keeping a healthcare record for the baby, and it would be wise to start this project in the group setting. Discuss the chapter summary and "When Do You Call the Doctor" handouts (pp. 69-70), and include a discussion of how to identify medical emergencies. The crossword puzzle is also a good addition to group activities.

Teaching Through Home Visits

Look at the activities and choose those you think best fit your client. You might even perform the "How Can I Help You, Baby?" reader theater (pp. 73-74) with you playing the role of Erin while your client plays Pati.

If possible, watch the "Keeping Your Baby Healthy" DVD with her. Also go over the "When Do You Call the Doctor?" (p. 70) and the "Health Care for Your Baby" (p. 69) handouts.

Help your client get started creating a healthcare record for her baby. Some moms keep this record in the car so it will be available when they take baby to the doctor. If she doesn't have a car, perhaps she will keep it in her baby bag or in her purse.

Your client might also enjoy working the "Illness and Prevention" crossword puzzle (p. 71), perhaps after your time with her is over. Or perhaps you will work it together.

Finding and using suitable learning activities to fit your teaching will greatly enhance the effectiveness of your guidance. Participants will enjoy your sessions with them more, and when we enjoy learning, that learning is far more long lasting.

Topic: Baby's Health
Your Baby's First Year
Chapter 4

Health Care for Your Baby — pp. 59-75

Objectives: Student will be able to

1. List the immunizations a baby needs to protect him/her from disease, including the age at which baby is to receive each one. (GRADS Competencies 3.3.16).

2. Describe techniques for preventing and treating diaper rash and caring for a colicky baby.

3. Describe techniques of caring for a sick child.

4. Identify strategies designed to keep a baby healthy. (GRADS 3.3.14, 6.2.1, 6.2.2, 6.2.3, 6.2.4)

SUPPLEMENTARY RESOURCES

Speaker. Medical person to recommend immunization schedule and to discuss the importance of having all children follow that schedule.

Video. Your Baby's First Year Series, Volume 4, "Keeping Baby Healthy." (Morning Glory Press)

TEACHER PREPARATION — CHAPTER 4

1. **Review Chapter 4,** text, pp. 59-75, and the workbook assignments and suggested responses, pp. 84-85 of this *Notebook.* Also review the quiz, p. 82, and quiz key, p. 83.

2. **Review the learning activities,** decide which ones you will use, and reproduce the needed handouts for students. Suggested for this chapter are: "Health Care for Your Baby," p. 76; "When Do You Call the Doctor?" p. 77; "Illness and Prevention" crossword puzzle, p. 78; Marlene's Journal — Evan's Cold, p. 79; Reader Theater, "How Can I Help You, Baby?" pp. 80-81; Video discussion guide, "Keeping Baby Healthy," p. 81-B; quiz over chapter 4, p. 82. **Write Baby Assignment on the board.**

3. **Schedule a healthcare provider** to discuss immunizations — recommended schedule, importance of, etc., as well as general health care of infants.

4. **Review video, "Keeping Your Baby Healthy,"** Volume 4, Your Baby's First Year Series. See video discussion guide, p. 81-B.

CORE CURRICULUM — GROUP LEARNING

Reading Assignment (individually or together)
Chapter 4, *Your Baby's First Year,* "Health Care for Your Baby," pp. 59-75. **Discuss.** Workbook questions (pp. 11-14) can guide discussion. **Optional:** Students write individual or group responses to questions. See pp. 84-85 for suggested responses to workbook assignments.

Reprinted with permission
*from **Your Baby's First Year Comprehensive Curriculum Notebook.***
Reduced to 60%. To reproduce at full size, enlarge to 150%.

LEARNING ACTIVITIES — CHAPTER 4

1. **Handout.** "Health Care for Your Baby," p. 76. Review together, then go on to next class discussion.

2. **Class Discussion.** Ask those who have had a sick baby or a baby with colic to discuss their experiences and share techniques they used to help baby be more comfortable.

3. **Speaker.** Medical person to recommend immunization schedule, discuss importance of having all children follow that schedule, health tips for babies, and when to call the healthcare provider.

4. **Video.** "Keeping Your Baby Healthy," Volume 4, Your Baby's First Year Series. See video discussion guide, p. 81-B.

5. **Reader Theater.** "How Can I Help You, Baby?" pp. 80-81. (Also assigned for *Challenge of Toddlers,* chapter 10.) Ask two students to read dramatically. Have a "sick" doll as a prop.

6. **Case Study.** Marlene's journal, p. 79 (reprinted from *Nurturing Your Newborn*, p. 69). Ask student to read as a dramatic monologue. She could move across stage to indicate a new day. Have a doll as a prop (assuming student's baby is not with her). If they were Marlene's friend, what could they tell her during the time Evan is sick with a cold? How could they help? Discuss possibilities.

7. **Writing Assignment.** Ask each student to write Marlene a note. Tell them to try to cheer her up during this difficult week.

8. **Journal.** Allow time for journals. Suggsted starter: "I met my boyfriend when I . . ."

9. **Puzzle.** "Illness and Prevention" crossword puzzle, p. 79. Work individually or in pairs, then discuss concepts illustrated in puzzle.

10. **Project. Health Care Record** (Workbook). Is each parent keeping a health record for her baby? If not, use class time to create the records. See pp. 62-63, text. (GRADS Competencies 3.3.17, 3.3.16) Each student should record baby's length and weight at birth and periodically thereafter. Write down baby's blood type and the immunizations s/he is given. Remind students to keep track of their child's illnesses by writing down the dates and a brief description of the symptoms.

11. **Writing Assignment** (Workbook). Ask students if their baby has been sick yet. If so, write a detailed report of her illness and how parent handled it. Tell them if their baby hasn't been sick, interview another parent who has had this experience. Write a report of the interview.

12. **Handout.** "When Do You Call the Doctor?" p. 77. Discuss, then ask students to place in their notebooks.

13. **Baby Assignment.** Choose a time when your baby is tired and fussy, perhaps not feeling well. Try several methods of soothing her. Describe your efforts in your journal.

14. **Quiz.** Chapter 4, p. 82. **Quiz key,** p. 83.

ENRICHMENT ACTIVITY — CHAPTER 4

Skit Writing/Role Play. As a small group or individually, ask students to write a skit about baby's first visit to the healthcare provider. The parent should get names of the receptionist and nurse, and should have a list of questions to ask the provider. Doctor is in a hurry, and student will need to say, "Wait, I have these questions and I need your help."

Reprinted with permission
*from **Your Baby's First Year Comprehensive Curriculum Notebook.***
Reduced to 60%. To reproduce at full size, enlarge to 150%.

INDEPENDENT STUDY ASSIGNMENTS — CHAPTER 4

Topic: Baby's Health
Your Baby's First Year

Resources
> Text: *Your Baby's First Year* and Workbook, Chapter 4.

Handouts
> "Health Care for Your Baby," p. 76.
> "When Do You Call the Doctor?" p. 77.
> "Illness and Prevention" crossword puzzle, p. 78.
> Marlene's Journal — Evan's Cold, p. 79
> Reader Theater: "How Can I Help You, Baby?" pp. 80-81.
> Video discussion guide, "Keeping Baby Healthy," p. 81-B.
> Quiz, Chapter 4, p. 82.

1. **Read Chapter 4**, *Your Baby's First Year,* "Health Care for Your Baby," pp. 59-75. Complete assignments in Workbook (pp. 11-14) including the writing assignment and the project.

2. **Handout.** "Health Care for Your Baby." Review, then place in your notebook.

3. **Write in your journal.** Suggsted starter: "I met my boyfriend when I . . ."

4. **Video.** Watch "Keeping Baby Healthy," and respond to discussion questions in writing.

5. **Reader Theater.** "How Can I Help You, Baby?" Read, then answer discussion questions in writing.

6. **Case Study.** Read the attached page from Marlene's journal (reprinted from *Nurturing Your Newborn,* p. 69). Then write Marlene a note. Try to cheer her up during this difficult week.

7. **Puzzle.** Work the "Illness and Prevention" crossword puzzle.

8. **Handout.** "When Do You Call the Doctor?" Review this information, then place the handout in your notebook.

9. **Baby Assignment.** Choose a time when your baby is tired and fussy, perhaps not feeling well. Try several methods of soothing her. Report the results in your journal.

10. **Quiz.** Please take the quiz over chapter 4.

Extra Credit:

Skit Writing/Role Play. Write a skit about a parent's first visit with baby to healthcare provider. In the skit, the parent will get the names of the receptionist and nurse. Mother or father will have a list of questions to ask the provider. Doctor is in a hurry, and parent will need to say, "Wait, I have these questions and I need your help."

Nurturing Your Newborn/Your Baby's First Year Comprehensive Curriculum Notebook   75

> *Reprinted with permission*
> *from **Your Baby's First Year Comprehensive Curriculum Notebook.***
> *Reduced to 60%. To reproduce at full size, enlarge to 150%.*

Prepared by Deborah Cashen, author of *Creating Parenting Notebooks*

Your Baby's First Year — Chapter 4

Health Care for Your Baby

COLIC

✓ No one knows what causes colic.

✓ It generally comes about the same time every day.

✓ Pick your baby up and provide comfort.

✓ Check with your doctor to make sure nothing else is wrong.

✓ By the time your baby is three months old she will probably grow out of it.

DIAPER RASH

✓ Best way to deal with diaper rash is to prevent it.

✓ Change your baby often.

✓ Try different diaper brands until you find one that seems right for your baby.

✓ Wash your baby with clean warm water or wipes when you change her.

IMMUNIZATIONS

✓ Immunizations are provided to protect your baby from childhood diseases.

✓ All of these diseases can cause death or very serious illness in children.

✓ Be sure you follow baby's immunization schedule the first 18 months.

✓ Keeping your regularly scheduled "well-baby" check-ups helps you stay on schedule.

At birth:	Hepatitis B
2 months:	HDTaP; hepatitis B; polio
4 months:	HDTaP; hepatitis B; polio
6 months:	HDTaP; hepatitis B; polio (can be later, up to 18 months)
12 – 15 months:	MMR, Varicella, TB skin test

HDTaP – *H. Influenzae, type b (Hib), Diptheria, Tetanus, Pertussis*
MMR – *Measles, mumps and rubella.*
Varicella – *Chickenpox*
TB – *Tuberculosis*

Prepared by Deborah Cashen, author of *Creating Parenting Notebooks*

Your Baby's First Year — Chapter 4

When Do You Call the Doctor?

CALL THE DOCTOR IF:

- ✓ Temperature, taken under the arm, is more than 101 degrees.
- ✓ She has a severe reaction to immunizations (high fever, rash, vomiting).
- ✓ Baby gets a sudden unexplained rash.
- ✓ After every feeding baby suddenly vomits most of his meal.
- ✓ Baby has diarrhea (thin, watery, foul-smelling discharge) more than 12 hours.
- ✓ You think baby may have a hernia (bulge around the navel or the seamline between the leg and tummy).
- ✓ You think baby has an ear infection.
- ✓ Baby has an eye infection, conjunctivitis (pink eye), which is very contagious.
- ✓ Baby has a skin infection (impetigo), also highly contagious.

MAKE SOME NOTES

- ✓ Is he coughing? For how long?
- ✓ Has he lost his appetite?
- ✓ Does he have diarrhea?
- ✓ What is his temperature?
- ✓ Has he been exposed to any diseases?
- ✓ Has he received the immunizations he should have had by this time?

HELPFUL HINTS

- ✓ Keep a record of your baby's immunizations.
- ✓ Don't give your child aspirin for fever unless directed by your doctor.
- ✓ Use a disposable or digital thermometer.
- ✓ Lukewarm baths help bring fevers down.
- ✓ Give baby plenty of liquids when he has a fever.
- ✓ Use age appropriate, non-aspirin pain relievers, such as Tylenol.
- ✓ When he's sick, keep your child at home. He benefits from not being exposed to other germs.

Your Baby's First Year, Chapter 4 (Edie De Avila)

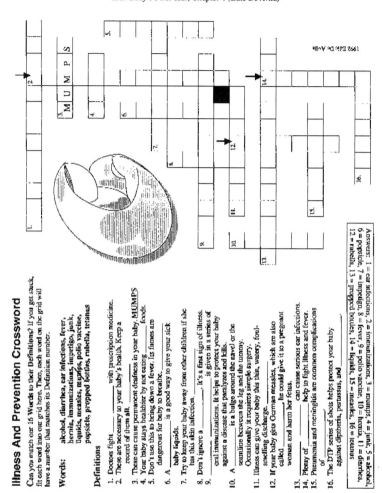

Illness And Prevention Crossword

Can you match our 16 Words to their Definitions? If you get stuck, fit each word into our grid here. Then, each word on the grid will have a number that matches its Definition number.

Words: alcohol, diarrhea, ear infections, fever, hernia, immunizations, impetigo, junk, liquids, measles, mumps, polio vaccine, popsicle, propped bottles, rubella, tetanus

Definitions

1. Doctors fight _____ with prescription medicine.
2. These are necessary to your baby's health. Keep a record of them all.
3. These can cause permanent deafness in your baby. MUMPS
4. Your baby stays healthier by not eating _____ foods.
5. Don't use this to bring down a fever. Its fumes are dangerous for baby to breathe.
6. A _____ is a good way to give your sick baby liquids.
7. Try to keep your baby away from other children if she has this skin infection.
8. Don't ignore a _____. It's a first sign of illness.
9. _____ is given in a series of oral immunizations. It helps to protect your baby against a disease that paralyzes and kills.
10. A _____ is a bulge around the navel or the seamline between the leg and the tummy. Occasionally it requires simple surgery.
11. Illness can give your baby this thin, watery, foul-smelling discharge.
12. If your baby gets German measles, which are also called _____ he could give it to a pregnant woman and harm her fetus.
13. _____ can cause serious ear infections.
14. Plenty of _____ help to fight illness and fever.
15. Pneumonia and meningitis are common complications of _____
16. The DTP series of shots helps protect your baby against diphtheria, pertussis, and _____

Answers: 1 = ear infections, 2 = immunizations, 3 = mumps, 4 = junk, 5 = alcohol, 6 = popsicle, 7 = impetigo, 8 = fever, 9 = polio vaccine, 10 = hernia, 11 = diarrhea, 12 = rubella, 13 = propped bottles, 14 = liquids, 15 = measles, 16 = tetanus.

1992 Edie De Avila

Your Baby's First Year, Chapter 4
Marlene's Journal — Evan's Cold

When Evan was three weeks old, he caught his first cold. Marlene, 15, kept a record of those days:

9/4: Today Evan has a slight cough. I hope it doesn't get worse.

9/5: Evan got the sniffles and his cough is worse. When I feed him, he'll cough, and it seems like he's choking. It scares me.

9/6: Evan's cold is getting worse. His nose is plugged. I called the doctor, and she told me to use normal saline and put it in his nose because he has a hard time breathing. I'm gonna take him to the doctor tomorrow because I want to make sure. My mom is helping me out.

9/8: Today Evan woke up around 9:00 and slept through most of the day. He's still coughing. His sniffles are getting a little better but he still gets plugged up from time to time. During the night, as usual, he's a grouch, but I finally got him to sleep by holding him in my arms and singing to him like I usually do.

9/9: Evan is a month old. He stays awake a lot. I don't mind that. It's the crying I could live without.

9/10: I wish his cold would go away. The doctor said we can't give him any medication because he's too young. I feel so sorry for him because it seems like he's having such a hard time.

9/12: He's still sick. He stays up so much, and he's always crying. I hate his cold. I don't have time these past few days to do anything because he's always awake and crying because he doesn't feel good.

9/14: Finally he's feeling better.

Writing Assignment. Do you have any suggestions that might make Evan or Marlene feel better? Write Marlene a note. Try to cheer her up during these difficult days.

Your Baby's First Year, Chapter 4
How Can I Help You, Baby?

Cast: Pati, Erin, and Erik. Pati's son, Erik, is four months old and has his first cold. Erin feels experienced in the art of helping a baby get through a cold — last month Cailin was miserable with a cold. Pati is dialing the phone.

Pati: Erin, what did you *do* when Cailin had that cold last month? I remember you said she was miserable, but what did you *do?* Poor little Erik. He's crying because he feels so bad, and the more he cries, the more stuffed up he is. I feel so helpless. I feel like crying with him. *(Pause)* You'll come over? Thanks a lot!

It's a few minutes later. The doorbell rings.

Pati: Come in, Erin. We're in the bedroom. *(Pati is rocking Erik, and both look miserable.)*

Erin: I'm glad you called when you did. Cailin just went to sleep, and Gram said she'd watch her. I'm not about to bring her over and get her started on another cold. It's too hard on both of us!

Pati: Do you think I should call the doctor?

Erin: Does he have a fever?

Pati: I haven't taken his temperature. I know he's having trouble breathing, and he can barely suck his bottle at all.

Erin: I think you should take his temperature. Do you have the kind of thermometer you can put under his arm? I brought mine in case you don't. Here, I'll show you. *(Erin shows Pati a digital thermometer, then puts it under Erik's arm.)* Now hold it there for one minute.

Pati: What can I do if he has a fever?

Erin: Ask your doctor if you can give him baby Tylenol. That's probably the best thing to do.

Pati: Mom's friend said if he ever gets a high fever, I should bathe him in alcohol.

Erin: Don't do it! Gram says people used to do that, but the fumes from alcohol are dangerous for the baby. It's better to bring his fever down by giving him a cooling bath. If he shivers while you bathe him, though, the water is too cold. You can put a towel in lukewarm water and wrap Erik in it. That helps bring fever down.

Pati: Look, he has a fever. This says 99°.

Erin: That's not bad, but you probably should tell his doctor. Is he able to take his bottle? He needs liquids when he's sick. When Cailin couldn't suck, I offered her a popsicle. I figured that much sugar wouldn't hurt her, and it was important she get some liquid. The doctor told me that was a good idea.

Pati: Erik looks so pathetic when his nose is all stuffed up like this.

Erin: Try putting a little normal saline in his nose. You can buy it at the drug store. It's a salty solution you use with a rubber syringe. That helps clear out the discharge. Oh, and do you have a cold-water vaporizer?

Pati: No. Should I?

Erin: Using one might help him breathe. I'll go get mine, and you can try it today. If his nose gets sore, put a little cream or ointment on it. That's soothing.

Pati: He's starting to cough, too.

Continued on next page

Reprinted with permission
*from **Your Baby's First Year Comprehensive Curriculum Notebook.***
Reduced to 60%. To reproduce at full size, enlarge to 150%.

How Can I Help You, Baby? — p. 2

Erin: Ask the doctor if you can get some kind of cough medicine.

Pati: Okay, I'll call the doctor. Seeing Erik like this is awful. What causes colds anyway? Is he going to have a lot of them?

Erin: How often he has colds depends on two things: first, if he's exposed to other people with colds — you notice I didn't bring Cailin over today. They don't need to be together when one of them has a cold. The other important thing is his own resistance to colds. Gram says if Cailin eats nutritious meals instead of junk foods and gets plenty of rest, she'll have fewer colds.

Pati: I'd do almost anything to prevent this.

Curtain

Discussion questions

1. Has your baby been sick yet? If so, describe his and your experience.

2. What are you doing to help your child stay as healthy as possible?

3. Why did Erin tell Pati to talk to the doctor before she gives Erik any medicine?

4. Why didn't Erin bring Cailin with her?

Your Baby's First Year Video Series
Discussion Questions

Volume 4 — Keeping Your Baby Healthy

1. List four series of immunizations your baby needs during her first year.

2. What should you do if your baby has a severe reaction, such as a high fever, after receiving an immunization?

3. List several signs, at least four, that may indicate your baby is allergic to something.

4. When you start to feed your baby solid food, how long should you wait after one new food before offering him another food he has never had before? Why?

5. Describe three things you can do to help your baby be more comfortable when he has a cold.

6. What can you do to help keep your baby from catching a cold?

7. If your baby is constipated, what might help him?

8. If your baby has diarrhea, what should you do?

9. What is a major cause of ear infections in babies?

Name _____

Your Baby's First Year Quiz – Chapter 4

TRUE/FALSE. Write "T" before the sentence if it is true. Write "F" before it if it is false.

____ 1. You can get free HDTaP shots for your baby at the Health Department.

____ 2. Most babies have some reaction to their immunizations.

____ 3. A hernia is a bulge around the navel or the seamline between the leg and the tummy.

____ 4. Most doctors don't want to see the baby until he's 3 months old.

____ 5. Popsicles are good for a child with fever.

____ 6. A good parent can keep his child from catching cold.

____ 7. With your doctor's help, you can cure your child's cold quickly.

____ 8. Most allergies in children under two are caused by foods.

____ 9. If your child has pink eye, it's okay to let him play around other children.

____ 10. Even if baby has a fever of 101 degrees, it's okay to ignore it if she's teething.

MULTIPLE CHOICE. Circle the letter of all correct answers.

11. Your infant is less likely to spit up if you
   a. give him frequent small feedings.
   b. feed him cereal at six weeks.
   c. lay him down and prop his bottle.
   d. handle him extra gently after feeding him.

12. If your baby has diarrhea,
   a. you don't need to do anything about it.
   b. give him clear liquids.
   c. feed him lots of cereal.
   d. give him Pedialyte.

13. If you think your child has an ear infection,
   a. ignore it.
   b. treat it yourself.
   c. call the doctor.
   d. prop his bottle when you feed him.

14. You can help your baby learn to talk by
   a. talking to her.
   b. reading to him.
   c. naming and describing things to him.
   d. all of the above.

15. At what age should your baby get her first HDTaP shots? _____

16. Where can you go for free immunizations for your baby? _____

17. Why is it extremely important that your child be given all of these immunizations?

18. Why is it important to keep a record of your baby's immunizations?

19-21. List three things you can do to bring your baby's fever down.
   1.
   2.
   3.

22-26. List five questions you should be able to answer when you call your doctor about your baby's condition.
   1.
   2.
   3.
   4.
   5.

27-29. List at least three things that might help a colicky baby feel better.
   1.
   2.
   3.

30-32. When should you call your baby's doctor? List three reasons.
   1.
   2.
   3.

Your Baby's First Year Quiz Key — Chapter 4

1 - T

2 - T

3 - T

4 - F

5 - T

6 - F

7 - F

8 - T

9 - F

10 - F

11 - a, d

12 - b, d

13 - c

14 - a, b, c, and/or d

15 - two months

16 - Public Health Department

17 - Because these diseases can cause death or very serious illness in children, each child needs to be immunized against them.

18 - Records are required when child enters school.

19-21 - Give him Tylenol, cooling bath, give him liquids.

22-26 - Five of the following: Is baby coughing? For how long? Has he lost his appetite? Does he have diarrhea? What is his temperature? Has he been exposed to any diseases? Has he had all the immunizations he should have had?

27-29 - Three of the following: holding him on his stomach across your knees, giving him a warm bath, holding him, doctor might prescribe medication.

30-32 - Three of the following: Baby's temperature is 101° or higher. Baby gets a sudden rash. He vomits most of his meal. He has diarrhea for 12 hours or more. She appears to have a hernia. Other responses may also be correct.

Your Baby's First Year — Chapter 4
Suggested Responses to Workbook Assignments

Health Care for Your Baby

Student Objectives

1. To list the immunizations a baby needs to protect him/her from disease.

2. To describe techniques of caring for a sick child.

Please read pages 59-75 and answer these questions.

1. What one term can be used to refer to a doctor, nurse practitioner, physician's assistant, or other health specialist? *Healthcare provider.*

2. Why is it a good idea to know the names of the people working in your baby's doctor's office?
If I call them by name when I telephone the office, I'm more likely to get a friendly response.

3. What should you do if your doctor is always in too much of a hurry to answer your questions?
*Write down everything I want to ask the doctor. When he appears to be in a hurry, I should stop him and say, "Wait, I have these questions. I need your help."
Then I would briefly describe whatever it is that's worrying me.*

4. Why should you keep a healthcare notebook in which you write down information about your baby's health and illnesses?
The notebook will help me communicate better with the healthcare provider.

5. What should your healthcare notebook include?
Baby's weight and length at birth and periodically thereafter; blood type and immunizations given; date and symptoms of illness.

6. Describe a baby who has colic.
He appears to have a stomach ache, and he will cry nearly every evening. His face may become red, he will frown, draw up his legs, and scream loudly.

7. What causes colic? *No one knows.*

8. What may help the colicky baby?
Holding him on his stomach across your knees; giving him a warm bath; doctor might prescribe medication.

9. How long does colic generally last?
Until the baby is about three months old.

10. How can you prevent diaper rash? *Change baby often. Wash her with clean water each time.*

11. Why is it important not to shake baby powder directly on baby?
Baby powder shaken in the air can hurt baby's lungs.

12. When a baby has a diaper rash, is it better to use a powder or an ointment to clear it up? Please explain.
During the day, the powder is best because you can wash it off each time you change her. At night the ointment is better because it gives longer protection.

13. At what age should your child start getting his HDTaP shots? *Two months.*
When should your baby be given polio vaccine?
At two months.

14. List four diseases covered by HDTaP immunizations.
Hib, diphtheria, tetanus, and pertussin.

15. Even if you've not known anyone with these diseases, why must you be sure your child gets immunized against them?
These diseases can cause death or very serious illness in children. I don't want to take that risk with my child.

16. What immunizations will your baby need when he's 15 months old?
Red measles, rubella, mumps, and chickenpox.

17. When should your child be immunized against chicken pox? *12-15 months.*

18. Where can you get free immunizations in *your* community? Call your Health Department to find out. Ask when and where you could take your baby to be immunized. *Personal response.*

19. If your baby has a slight fever for a day or two after she gets her shots, how can you help her feel better?
Give her a non-aspirin pain reliever.

20. Why should you keep a record of your baby's immunizations?
You'll need the record when you enroll him in school.

21. Describe the best way to take baby's temperature.
Put a disposable or digital thermometer under her arm.

22. If your baby spits up after being fed, what might help prevent this?
Feed him less food more often. Handle him extra gently after feeding him.

23. List at least five reasons to call your baby's healthcare provider.
1. Baby's temperature is 101° or higher.
2. Baby gets a sudden rash.
3. He vomits most of his meal.
4. He has diarrhea for 12 hours or more.
5. She appears to have a hernia.
(Student may include other reasons.)

24. List six pieces of information you should have when you call your baby's doctor.
1. Is baby coughing? For how long?
2. Has he lost his appetite?

Your Baby's First Year — Chapter 4 — Cont.
Suggested Responses to Workbook Assignments

1. Is baby coughing? For how long?
2. Has he lost his appetite?
3. Does he have diarrhea?
4. What is his temperature?
5. Has he been exposed to any diseases?
6. Has he had all the immunizations he should have had by this time?

25. If the doctor prescribes antibiotics for your child, should you continue giving the baby the medicine until it's gone even if she's feeling better? *Yes.*

26. Why is it dangerous for baby to have diarrhea for very long? *She can lose a dangerous amount of fluid.*

What's the best way to treat diarrhea?
Give the baby clear liquids and nothing else for 24 hours. Liquids should include Pedialyte.

27. What is a hernia?
A bulge around the navel or the seamline between the leg and the tummy.

What will the doctor probably suggest if the hernia does not go away? *Surgery to remove the hernia.*

28. If your child has a fever, what can you do about it? *Give the baby non-aspirin pain reliever if the doctor says it's okay. Give baby a cooling bath or wrap her in a towel wrung out of lukewarm water. Give her liquids.*

29. Someone may tell you to bathe your child in alcohol when she has a high fever. Why is this not a good idea? *Alcohol fumes could hurt baby.*

30. How can popsicles help a child who has a fever? *He will get liquid from the popsicle.*

Is it also a good idea to give baby popsicles if he's vomiting? *Yes.*

31. What should you do if your baby's ears appear to hurt her?
Take her to the doctor. There is a danger of permanent hearing loss if an ear infection is not treated promptly.

32. Has your baby had a cold yet? *Personal response.*

33. If your baby has a cold, what can you do to make him feel more comfortable when he has the following symptoms:
He has a fever or a headache: *Tylenol may help.*

She has a runny nose: *Clean the discharge from her nose with a rubber syringe and normal saline.*
He has a stuffy nose: *Use a cold water vaporizer.*
She appears congested: *Decongestant medicine might help.*
He's coughing: *Give her cough medicine if the doctor says it's okay.*
She doesn't want to eat: *Encourage him to drink juice, water, clear soups, weak tea.*

34. What can you do to help your child stay in good health? *See that he eats nutritious meals instead of junk foods, and that he gets plenty of rest.*

35. What seems to be the cause of most allergies in children under two? *Certain foods.*

36. What effect may second-hand smoke have on a child? *Child may develop asthma and other allergies.*

36. When do most doctors start allergy testing? *When the child starts school.*
Why do they wait this long? *Many allergies disappear as baby grows.*

37. Should a child with pink eye or impetigo be around other children? *No.* Why or why not? *Other children can catch these diseases from her.*

Writing Assignment

Has your baby been sick yet? If so, write a detailed report of her illness and how you handled it. If she hasn't been sick, interview another mother who has had this experience. Write a report of your interview.

Project

Keep a record of your baby's health as described on page 63, text. Record your baby's height and weight at birth and periodically thereafter. Write down your baby's blood type and the immunizations s/he is given. Keep track of your child's illnesses by writing down the dates and a brief description of the symptoms. Attach your record to assignment, but ask your teacher to return it.

Take the quiz over chapter 4.

She's learning and she loves it as Daddy reads to her.

3

Reading for Life — Parent *and* Child

Promoting literacy for two generations simultaneously — what a wonderful challenge!

If you teach in a school program, you know this is a major goal of any educational setting. If you lead a weekly or monthly group of teen parents, or you teach parenting through home visits or another one-on-one setting, however, you realize it wouldn't make sense to ask your clients to read during the short time you're with them. If you don't or can't offer school credit for outside reading, what incentive is there?

First of all, some teens like to read. Many teens enjoy reading *if* they are interested in the topic and if the material is truly reader-friendly, i.e., keeps their interest as they read.

Second, reading to one's child is a big part of parenting well. If you have self-proclaimed non-readers among your clients, encourage them to read picture books to their children. (What other group of teens could we ask to read picture books without insulting them?) Help them find books that their children will enjoy.

Encourage them to go to the library, get a library card, and check books out regularly.

> *I read to Shelly. I think that helps her learn to talk. I*
> *started reading to her when she was ten months old.*
> *I don't like to read unless it's what I want to read.*
> *But when I read to Shelly, I know what I'm getting out*
> *of it. I enjoy it. And she starts mumbling as though she's*
> *reading. That's how she learned the name doggie, etc.*
> *She turns the pages herself.*
>
> Dixie, 18 – Shelly, 17 months

Children who are read to tend to be better readers, thus preparing them to succeed in school. The bedtime reading routine needs to start *early.*

Is there a collection of children's books in your classroom or meeting place? If you're a home visitor, perhaps your car can be turned into a little bookmobile, and your clients can check out books regularly. Even if you don't have easy access to a public library, parent and child can choose their books together.

Some parents might like to start with picture books with no words, such as the beautifully illustrated, almost wordless Carl books by Alexandra Day. See bibliography. The parent can tell the story — until the baby is old enough to join in the telling. Check your local or Internet book store for other titles.

Occasionally demonstrate reading a children's book with drama. Perhaps you'll devote one group session to sharing books your clients liked when they were little. Ask each participant to read a short book to the others. (When asked to read aloud, participants need to be able to pass up the opportunity if they choose.)

If you're teaching one on one, a reading session with your client's child could be valuable to both parent and child.

Several national programs focus on reading to children. Reading Is Fundamental, Inc. (RIF®) offers a Shared Beginnings® literacy program for teen parents and their children. The program promotes parental involvement in their child's language and literacy development and provides a foundation for continued literacy development in parents. Both parents and children select books to keep, and RIF provides programs with materials and resources to promote involvement and bonding through literacy.

To apply to run a RIF program or for more information, email <contactus@rif.org>

Susan Straub's READ TO ME program is a series of workshop activities which can be offered in any order. The program is easily adapted for whatever time is available, i.e., within a 40-minute classroom period, or 1-3 hours after school, or even on a Saturday morning at the local community center.

See Straub's website for more information — **<www.readtomeprogram.org>** or call 212.691.6590, x 26, or email <Susan@readtomeprogram.org>

For funding, check with your local service organizations (Lions Club, Rotary, Soroptomist, etc.). They may have small grants available for projects such as these.

Never forget your local library. The children's librarian is a wonderful resource. Ask her/him to talk to your group about reading to children, and to bring examples of good books for babies, toddlers, and preschoolers with her/him.

Making Books

Making a book for one's child is a fun activity. Encourage participants to illustrate their books themselves, but also provide magazines with lots of colorful pictures from which they can cut their illustrations if they prefer. Photos of the child, family members, and pets make wonderful illustrations.

First, talk about what their children are interested in at this time. During the first year, big bright illustrations of things they know — the cat and dog, chair, table, etc. — are good starters. The toddler would love a story about herself — "This Is Amy's Day" is a great topic.

Laminating the pages of the books provides good protection. If this is not feasible, make the pages of light cardboard and cut to the size of plastic sandwich bags. Insert the page, punch holes in the left side, and tie together with a short piece of heavy yarn or cord. (A longer piece of cord can be a dangerous toy.)

As the child begins to talk, he'd like a *"Book of _____'s Words."*

Developing a Life-Long Reading Habit

One of the greatest goals language arts/English teachers may set for students is that they develop a life-long reading habit. However, according to an Associated Press/Ipsos poll, one in four U.S. adults said they had read *no* books in 2006. The typical person claimed to have read four books in the last year — half read more and half read fewer. Another source (eContent magazine, 11/04) reports that for every three adults who read a book in 2002, two did not. The life-long reading habit does not come automatically.

Is this a problem, or simply the way it's supposed to be? Well, those of us who enjoy reading are a little sad about all those people missing out on the joy of reading.

Does this have anything to do with parenting? I certainly think so. Reading expands one's horizons, provides a broader outlook on life, and, quite simply, adds to the joys of living. And this adds to one's parenting ability.

True, parents of babies and toddlers tend not to have much time for reading. In fact, throughout their children's growing-up years, the responsibilities of parenting and of earning a living leave little time for extra reading. On the other hand, how do these same people find time to watch TV? What if the parent who comes home each evening exhausted, and collapses in front of the TV, had learned to read for pleasure? Might reading be real competition for the often-mindless TV show?

Reading is important. To succeed at school, one must read. Most jobs require at least some reading. One's reading skills are likely to improve the more one reads. Reading Shakespeare is fine, but for good or bad, many teens consider Shakespeare something one reads only when required to do so. They read Shakespeare because it matters in their work toward high school credit. Many teens will read if it matters.

When you give your students a pamphlet about parenting, you hope they read it. But will they read *books* about parenting? Might they even *enjoy* reading these books?

Many teachers report that their students actually like to read the books in the *Teens Parenting* Series. The regular edition is written at a sixth grade reading level, the reading level of most newspapers.

Concepts are illustrated with verbatim quotes from young people dealing with the situation being discussed. Photos of teen parents are used throughout the books.

For young parents who find reading especially difficult, an easier reading edition of some of the books is available (*Your Pregnancy and Newborn Journey, Nurturing Your Newborn, Your Baby's First Year*, and *Discipline from Birth to Three*). This edition contains the same information, and the same photos and quotes from teen parents, but the information is presented at a second grade reading level (Flesch Grade Level Formula). Workbooks and answer keys are also available at this reading level. For more information about this curriculum, see p. 181-182.

Students learning English as a second language will find this easier reading edition a useful bridge to learning to read English at a higher level.

The *Teens Parenting* books are available in Spanish along with workbooks and teacher answer keys in Spanish.

Teaching Concepts Through Fiction

Do you use fiction much in your teaching? Sometimes a short story or a novel can get a point across better than a "real" textbook. Another reason to utilize fiction in your teaching is that reading absorbing novels can turn an "I won't read" teen into an individual who finds joy in reading.

Whether you're teaching English or language arts, or you simply realize the strengths of teaching concepts through fiction, you'll appreciate Marilyn Reynolds' True to Life Series from Hamilton High. The nine novels and one book of short stories all deal with teen crises.

Start with *Detour for Emmy*, the story of a 15-year-old who has a baby. Thousands of pregnant teens have read and enjoyed *Detour for Emmy*. Many have written to the author sharing their own experiences and telling Reynolds how much they relate to Emmy.

Baby Help is about Melissa who lives with Rudy, their baby, and Rudy's mother. Melissa doesn't think she is abused because Rudy only hits her when he's drinking . . . Melissa's story may help another teen manage to get out of an abusive relationship.

The best choice for a teen dad is *Too Soon for Jeff*, a novel about a reluctant teen father. *Beyond Dreams* includes six short stories dealing with situations faced by teenagers — drinking and driving, racism, school failure, abortion, partner abuse, aging relative. Three of the protagonists are male.

One of Reynolds' latest books (2007) is *No More Sad Goodbyes*. After a tragedy leaves Autumn with no living relatives, she must decide whether to abort (already too late), keep, or place for adoption the baby growing inside her after a one-time mistake with her best friend's heartthrob. Reynolds is also the author of *Shut Up!, Love Rules, If You Loved Me, But What About Me?* and *Telling*. All are realistic, teen-centered novels. Even "non-reading" teens report reading her books. See bibliography for more information.

Other excellent novels with teen parent themes include *True Believer* and *Make Lemonade* by Virginia Euwer, *Waiting for June* by Joyce Sweeney, *The First Part Last* by Angela Johnson, and *Imani All Mine* by Connie Porter. See bibliography.

Help your students develop a love of poetry by offering *The Softer Side of Hip-Hop: Poetic Reflections on Love, Family, and Relationships* by Laura Haskins-Bookser, a former teen mom. Laura shares her pain, frustrations, and joys as she parents her child. It's an honest look at the realities of early parenthood. A teacher's guide is available.

Haskins-Bookser is also the author of *Dreams to Reality: Help for Young Moms — Education, Career and Life Choices*. The journal for the book allows the reader to ponder how the ideas and concepts presented apply to her own life.

Another valuable book to offer young parents is *Breaking Free from Partner Abuse: Voices of Battered Women Caught in the Cycle of Domestic Violence* by Mary Marecek. Reading it can help an abused woman realize she is not alone, and that she can get help.

For-Credit Course

If your students receive credit for completing your parenting course, whether in the classroom or through independent study, you will find the parenting texts and the workbook assignments an important part of the curriculum. The chapter questions help students pull out essential information as they read. Strongly encourage them to think of their own child as they read and complete assignments.

They are not simply learning about caring for babies and toddlers. They are learning more about their own child. What a wonderful learning incentive!

While it is not really possible to test one's parenting abilities simply through written questions and answers, the quizzes are a useful part of the course evaluation. Perhaps you will decide to ask them to take the quiz before reading the material, and again after reading and discussing the information. This will help you determine whether they learn new things as they study.

Quiz results can also help you evaluate your teaching. Whether or not you use the quiz as a pre-test, poor results at the end of the testing period could mean you want to consider additional ways to present the information.

How Much Reading?

If you plan for your class to spend a week on a chapter topic, start by introducing the concepts. Then allow time for students to read at least some of the chapter. As you encourage students to read about parenting, rather, about their babies, usually a high interest topic for teen parents, you'll also be encouraging literacy.

If you have students who don't like to read or don't read well, you'll need a variety of approaches. One week, take turns reading, perhaps with different students playing the parts of the teens quoted in the chapter.

Another time divide the class into groups of two or three. Give each group a different section of the chapter. Tell them to read their section and answer the workbook questions over that section. Later, in class discussion, each student will be an expert on the section s/he read.

Or you can put the workbook questions on cards. Divide students into pairs to answer the questions.

The workbook questions can be used as guides for class discussion whether or not the students respond to each question in writing. All workbook assignments include ideas for writing, most of which are reproduced in the Learning Activities sections of the *Comprehensive Curriculum Notebooks.*

The workbooks also include many research projects, and most of these, too, are included in the *Comprehensive Curriculum Notebooks* for use in the classroom. Suggested responses for all workbook assignments are included in each chapter section of the notebook.

If you want to test your students on their understanding of the chapter materials, you'll find the quizzes and answer keys in the appropriate chapter sections of the *Notebooks.*

Improving Writing Skills

If you encourage your students to answer each workbook question in complete sentences and always to use good grammar, punctuation, and spelling, their writing skills may also improve as they complete these assignments as well as the writing and other learning activities for each chapter.

Each chapter in the Workbook and the learning activities in the Notebook for each chapter include several specific writing assignments. A good approach is to assign two grades to these assignments, one for the information contained in the paragraph or essay, and another for the neatness, grammar, spelling, punctuation, and sentence and paragraph structure of the writing.

Students who need help in mastering basic reading and writing skills can practice those skills as they complete the workbook assignments and other learning activities. With adequate coaching, the student's skills should improve appreciably, especially if all responses are checked for spelling, punctuation, sentence structure, etc. The best way to teach spelling is to expect the student to learn to spell correctly the misspelled words in his/her assignments.

Writing assignments can evolve into a class newsletter. Topics could include care of the newborn, dealing with baby's illness, handling the stresses of parenting, coping with a one-year-old, joys of parenting, etc. Developing an attractive format with lots of white space and easy-to-read articles encourages reading.

The newsletter can be used to publicize current parenting teen events. You and your students might even develop a newsletter for distribution beyond the classroom — to former and/or potential students or simply as a way to publicize your program.

Reading with No School Credit?

Is reading necessary for non-credit groups? Probably not as a requirement, but that can be an advantage. Teens may read more willingly if it is a choice, providing they consider the material truly interesting and worth their time.

If you see your clients once a week, or perhaps only once a month, you will probably have some participants who choose not to read — perhaps because they don't read well, because they have to read so much in school, because they lack time for "just reading," or simply because they are convinced they hate reading.

This doesn't mean you forget about suggesting reading material. Acquire a mini-library of parenting books, and offer checkout privileges. Be alert to what's going on with individual parents and their children. Did someone comment about her child's imaginary play? Suggest she read chapter 4 in *Challenge of Toddlers*, "Her Imagination Soars." (This is the chapter for which the activities are reproduced on pp. 93-101.) Is someone talking about the sudden independence his child is exhibiting? He might like to read the chapter on this topic. Become familiar with the various topics covered in each book. These are probably most of the same topics you cover in your group sessions. This will help you make inviting reading suggestions to the individuals in your group.

Teaching in the Classroom

The chapter assignment reprint here is from *The Challenge of Toddlers Comprehensive Curriculum Notebook*, chapter 4, "Her Imagination Soars." All speakers and activities would be appropriate for classroom teaching. To prepare, schedule a children's librarian to share picture books with your class and to inspire parents to read to their children often.

Also invite a caregiver from a daycare center. Ask her to bring along a toddler, then demonstrate reading to the child.

You might also obtain a variety of picture books for class

research on sexism in children's books (enrichment activity #1).

If you use the Nursery Rhyme game, you need to gather clues for it as well as materials for making a picture book for a child (activity #9, p. 99).

Your week of classroom lesson plans might include:

Monday. Start with the infant center caregiver reading to a toddler. Students may be surprised at how much a toddler loves to have someone read to him.

Spend the rest of the period reading the chapter, independently or as a group. If you want students to complete assignments in the workbook, perhaps you will ask pairs of students to work on specific sections, then be ready to share their learning on Tuesday.

Tuesday. Give each student the chapter summary handout (p. 96), and discuss. Then share the hints for reading to a child (activity #5, p. 98). Ask young parents to follow these hints with their own child, and report the results. Or cut apart the hints, and give one to each participant. Ask him/her to read the hint, then talk about it. Have they tried some of these suggestions with their children? Which ones worked?

Note there is a chart at the bottom of the page for entering the title and author of each book read to the child, together with the date of reading.

Wednesday. Most babies and toddlers love to hear nursery rhymes. Yet you may find your teen clients are not familiar with the old rhymes. On p. 99, you'll find "Nursery Rhyme Game Reinforces Reading to Child." For this game, each participant is given a sheet of nursery rhyme titles together with a clue list. Clues — small symbols representing each rhyme — need to be hidden throughout the room.

Perhaps you will print out the nursery rhymes and post them around the room. If the clue list is separate from the title list, the game will be more challenging.

A good before-game session might be devoted to students taking turns reading the designated rhymes aloud.

Thursday. Ask a children's librarian to share picture books with your students and inspire them to read to their children often.

Friday. Picture book assignment (enrichment activity #1). Supply a stack of children's books suitable for children under 3 years. Ask students to check books for sexist comments and illustrations.

Or

Let students each make a *Book of (Your Child)'s Words* (enrichment activity #2). Use light cardboard for the pages. Punch holes in the pages and tie them together with yarn. Find pictures to represent the words the child is saying. Tell each student to read the book to her child.

See the other activity suggestions described on p. 94.

If you are a for-credit independent study teacher or you need make-up assignments for students, see Independent Study Assignments on p. 95. These can also be learning assignments for part of your class while you interact with the others.

Not-for-Credit Groups

To begin your group session, follow the Discussion starter activity (#1) — ask students to share memories of their own childhood, then discuss the handout, "Your Child's Imagination Soars" (p. 96).

Ask each parent to observe her/his child closely after school, watching for situations in which the child mimics the parent. Then discuss at the following session.

Go over the "Hints for Reading to a Child" (p. 98) with your group. Ask them to keep a record on this handout of the books they read to their children. Encourage them to keep track of the number of times/amount of time they read to their child the following week, then report to the group.

Discuss how parents help their child learn to talk, and how reading to their child enhances language development.

Play the Nursery Rhyme Game (p. 99). Will participants help you find the props?

Bring a toddler in for part of your session and demonstrate reading to him. Some of the participants may not have had much experience in reading to small children. As mentioned above, perhaps a teacher from a daycare program would bring a child and perform this demonstration.

Provide supplies for participants to make books for their children. Emphasize how much their child would like a story about his/her activities. Or perhaps write a story about the pets they have at home.

Bring books — parenting and fiction — to your session and give a brief book talk. Briefly describe them to your clients and ask if they would like to check out one or two.

As mentioned before, if you don't have funding for books, approach a service club — Lions, Rotary, Soroptomists, etc. — and ask for a small grant to buy books for your group of young parents.

Reading and Home Visits

As suggested before, have copies of parenting books available to loan to your clients. Suggest s/he read a chapter between your visits, then begin the next visit with a brief discussion of that chapter. You may be surprised at the young parents who read *if it matters*.

Most of the above activities work well one-on-one. Any of the discussion topics listed above are valuable for individual conversation, too. Combine the "Hints for Reading to a Child" (p. 98) with a discussion about the wonderful benefits of reading frequently (every day) to one's child. Then ask the young parent to demonstrate reading to her child — or, if she doesn't want to do that, you demonstrate the reading.

Ask your client to make a picture book for her child, and show it to you at your next visit. You may want to bring supplies you think she might not easily find herself. Or perhaps you and your client will make the book together.

Have some books available to describe to your client, and suggest she check out her choice.

Perhaps you can get a grant from a service club for gift certificates to a local bookstore. Have several home-visit parents and children meet at the bookstore to pick out books together.

As you help your clients develop the reading habit, both for themselves and for their children, you will be adding greatly to the quality of their lives.

Topic: Toddler's Imagination
The Challenge of Toddlers

Chapter 4

Her Imagination Soars — pp. 56-65

Objectives: Student will be able to

1. Give three examples of the toddler's intense desire to mimic and to "help" her parent.

2. List three techniques for helping a toddler learn to talk.

SUPPLEMENTARY RESOURCES

Speaker. Children's librarian.

Picture Books for class project.

Clues for Nursery Rhyme game (p. 52).

Special Guests. Toddler with caregiver to demonstrate reading to child.

TEACHER PREPARATION — CHAPTER 4

1. **Review Chapter 4,** text, pp. 56-65, and the workbook assignments and suggested responses, p. 54 of this *Notebook.*

2. **Review the learning activities,** decide which ones you will use, and reproduce the needed handouts for students. Suggested for this chapter are: "Your Child's Imagination Soars," p. 49; "Hints for Reading to a Child," p. 51; "Amazing Toddlers" puzzle, p. 50; "Plastic Sieve for Water Play," p. 53. Also read "Nursery Rhyme Game Reinforces Reading to Child," p. 52. **Write the Parent/ Child Assignment on the board.**

3. **Schedule a children's librarian** to share picture books with your class and to inspire parents to read to their children frequently.

4. **Obtain a variety of picture books** for class research on sexism in children's books.

5. **Invite a caregiver from a daycare center and a toddler** to demonstrate reading to a child.

6. **Review suggestions for Nursery Rhyme game,** p. 52. Gather clues in preparation for playing the game.

7. **Obtain materials for making** *Book of (Your Child)'s Words* — light cardboard, hole punch, glue, marking pens, heavy yarn.

CORE CURRICULUM — GROUP LEARNING

Reading Assignment (individually or together)
Chapter 4, *The Challenge of Toddlers,* "Her Imagination Soars," pp. 56-65. **Discuss.** Workbook questions (pp. 9-10) can guide discussion. **Optional:** Students write individual or group responses to questions. See p. 54 for suggested responses to workbook assignments.

LEARNING ACTIVITIES — CHAPTER 4

1. **Discussion Starter** (adapted from Workbook). Ask students to share memories of their own pretend play as children — and/or pretend play they have observed in other children. Include accounts of toddlers mimicking and "helping" their parents. Then discuss **handout,** "Your Child's Imagination Soars," p. 49.

2. **Writing Assignment** (Workbook). Ask students to write an essay discussing a child's pretend play. Did they ever have an imaginary friend? Ask them to share their memories.

3. **Special Assignment.** Ask each parent to observe her child closely after school. Watch for situations in which the child mimics the parent. It's okay to make a special effort to do things the child might mimic: making faces, crawling on the floor, making sounds, etc. Ask each student to report results. Make a list on the chalkboard of different ways children mimic their parents. Then discuss what this means in terms of guiding and teaching their children.

4. **Speaker.** Ask a children's librarian to share picture books with your students and inspire them to read to their children frequently.

5. **Handout/Discussion.** Give each student "Hints for Reading to a Child," p. 51. Discuss, and ask students to keep a record in their notebooks of the books they read to their child.

6. **Puzzle.** "Amazing Toddlers," p. 50. Suggest that students work in pairs to complete the puzzle. Then discuss the concepts illustrated by the puzzle.

7. **Class Discussion/Writing Assignment.** Discuss how parents can help their children learn to talk. Follow by asking students to describe in writing at least three things they're doing to help their children learn to talk.

8. **Journal.** Suggested starter: "I worry a lot about . . ."

9. **Nursery Rhyme Game.** Play the game, "Nursery Rhyme Game Reinforces Reading to Child," p. 52. Perhaps students will help you collect props for the game.

10. **Reading Demonstration.** Ask someone to bring a toddler to class (preferably 12-18 months old) and demonstrate reading to the child. Then encourage students to discuss their reading experiences with their children.

11. **Parent/Child Assignment.** Make a box of dress-up clothes for your child. Include a hat made from a plastic bottle. See p. 53. Or make him a water sieve.

ENRICHMENT ACTIVITIES

1. **Picture Book Assignment.** Bring a stack of children's books to class, mostly picture books suitable for children aged 12-24 months. Ask students to check books for sexist comments and illustrations. Discuss the problem in expecting little girls to behave one way (generally less active) and little boys another (generally very active).

2. *Book of (Your Child)'s Words.* Use light cardboard for the pages. Punch holes in the pages and tie them together with yarn. Find pictures to represent the words your child is saying, "Ma-ma," "Da-da," "Bye," and "Dog" may be his first understandable words. Put a picture of each in the book, then read it with him. Soon he may be "reading" the pictures to you.

INDEMENDENT STUDY ASSIGNMENTS — CHAPTER 4

Topic: Toddler's Imagination
The Challenge of Toddlers

Resources
Text: *The Challenge of Toddlers* **and Workbook, Chapter 4.**

Handouts
"Your Child's Imagination Soars," p. 49.
"Hints for Reading to a Child," p. 51.
"Amazing Toddlers" puzzle, p. 50.
"Toys for Your Toddler — Dress-Up Clothes, Play Hats, Plastic Sieve for Water Play," p. 53.

1. **Read Chapter 4,** *The Challenge of Toddlers,* "Her Imagination Soars," pp. 56-65. Complete assignments in Workbook (pp. 9-10) including writing assignment and project.

2. **Handout.** "Your Child's Imagination Soars." Review, then place in your notebook.

3. **Write in your journal.** Suggested starter: "I worry a lot about . . ."

4. **Special Assignment.** Observe your child closely. Watch for situations in which s/he mimics you. It's okay to make a special effort to do things your child might mimic: making faces, crawling on the floor, making sounds, etc. In writing, report on the results and discuss what this means in terms of guiding and teaching your child.

5. **Reading Record.** Review "Hints for Reading to a Child." For the rest of this semester, keep a record in your notebook of the books you read to your child.

6. **Puzzle.** Complete the **"Amazing Toddlers"** puzzle.

7. **Writing Assignment.** Describe the things you can do to help your child learn to talk. Include at least three ways, and preferably more.

8. **Parent/Child Assignment.** Make a box of dress-up clothes for your child. Include a hat made from a plastic bottle. See attached directions. Or make him a water sieve.

*Reprinted with permission
from **The Challenge of Toddlers
Comprehensive Curriculum Notebook.**
Reduced to 60%. To reproduce at full size, enlarge to 150%.*

Prepared by Deborah Cashen, author of *Creating Parenting Notebooks*

The Challenge of Toddlers — Chapter 4

Your Child's Imagination Soars

ENCOURAGE YOUR TODDLER'S IMAGINATION

✓ Children this age love to pretend.

✓ Toddlers love to help you clean, cook, or pick up around the house.

✓ When you talk, pronounce words correctly and clearly. Don't correct him.

✓ Encourage him to say words without frustrating him.

✓ Expect one- or two-word sentences.

✓ When reading, the pictures are more important than the words.

✓ Choose books with bright, simple pictures.

✓ Provide lots of variety in your child's books.

✓ Books about familiar topics are more likely to keep your toddler's interest.

✓ Look for books that show boys and girls, men and women, as human beings with lots of different abilities and interests.

✓ **You are your child's most important teacher. He will learn far more interacting with you during this stage than he ever will again!**

> **When you read to your child and encourage his imagination, you're laying the foundation for reading and other successful school experiences for him later.**

The Challenge of Toddlers, Chapter 4 (Edie De Avila)

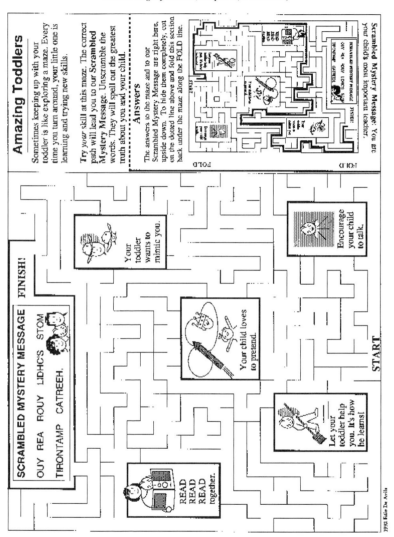

*Reprinted with permission
from **The Challenge of Toddlers
Comprehensive Curriculum Notebook.**
Reduced to 60%. To reproduce at full size, enlarge to 150%.*

The Challenge of Toddlers, Chapter 4

Hints for Reading to a Child

*The following list was developed for Families for Literacy by Beth Boxer,
Contra Costa, California, Family Library.*

- Read to your child anytime and any place: at the bus stop, while waiting at the doctor's office, while s/he is in the bath.

- Start with short reading sessions, and slowly build up to longer sessions.

- Pick a time when your child is calm. Try the same time each day.

- Find a comfortable and quiet place away from the TV and phone.

- Let your child sit close to you or on your lap.

- Follow the words with your finger.

- Let your child turn the pages.

- Make this a fun time. Enjoy the story and your child. Ask questions about the pictures and the story. Let your child ask questions, too.

- Try making your voice get loud, soft, fast and slow to make the story interesting.

- If your child gets bored or fussy, try a different book or a different time.

- Review books with your child by looking at the cover and pictures.

- Read the title, author's and illustrator's names.

- Point out pictures, shapes, colors and page numbers.

- At the end of the story ask who, what, when, why and how questions.

- Read favorite books more than once.

- "Read" wordless books to your child. Let your child "read" them to you.

- Show your child different types of reading material: cookbooks, comic strips, science books, magazines, and joke books.

Books I Have Read to My Child					
Date	**Title**	**Author**	**Date**	**Title**	**Author**

Please continue your list in your notebook. *Most important,* read to your child *every day!*

The Challenge of Toddlers, Chapter 4

Nursery Rhyme Game Reinforces Reading to Child

Game developed by Jeannette Lewis, Project PARENT,
Central Susquehanna (Pennsylvania) Intermediate Unit.

Give each student a sheet of nursery rhyme titles together with a clue list. Clues — small symbols representing each rhyme — are hidden throughout the room.

For example, someone finds the candle and realizes this is the symbol for "Jack Be Nimble." Each parent finds a designated number of clues, and decides which rhymes they match. Each individual shows their clues, and everyone says or reads the rhyme as a group.

The game is likely to be more exciting if each

parent is then allowed to choose a book for their child. Some teen parent programs have received grants for this purpose from a local service club or other source.

Possibilities might be your local Lions or Kiwanis Club, Soroptomist Club, or other service organization, or perhaps a local church would like to donate good children's books.

The goal of this game, of course, is to encourage young parents to read to their children. Reading nursery rhymes is a great start.

Find the Clues

Old King Cole — crown

Hey, Diddle Diddle — spoon

Three Men in a Tub — tub

Twinkle, Twinkle, Little Star — star

Baa, Baa, Black Sheep — 3 bags

Little Boy Blue — horn

Mary Had a Little Lamb — lamb

Three Little Kittens — mittens

Hickory Dickory Dock — clock

Little Miss Muffet — spider

Three Blind Mice — knife

Peter, Peter, Pumpkin Eater — pumpkin

Jack Be Nimble — candle

Humpty, Dumpty — egg

The Old Woman in a Shoe — shoe

Jack and Jill — pail

Mary, Mary, Quite Contrary — flowers

The Challenge of Toddlers, Chapter 4

Toys for Your Toddler

Dress-Up Clothes

Toddlers enjoy dressing up in bigger clothes. This activity helps promote imaginative play. It also helps them learn self-help skills. Size 4 shirts and sweaters, short petticoats with elastic waists, adult size socks that stretch and will easily pull on over bare feet or shoes are all fun for your child's dressing-up times.

Play hats may also add to the fun.

Play Hats

These make durable hats for dress-up time.

Materials:
• One-gallon plastic bottle
• Brightly colored yarn

Procedure:
Cut the bottle off about four inches from the bottom. Contour it into an interesting shape—scallops, duck bill, etc.

Overcast the edge and decorate with yarn. (A heavy needle will go through the plastic easily.)

Plastic Sieve for Water Play

Materials:
• Plastic milk jug
• Ice-pick

Procedure:
Cut the top half off the jug.
Poke holes in the lower half with an ice-pick.
Be very careful not to leave the ice-pick where a child can get it.
Let your child play with his sieve in the bathtub or other water.

The Challenge of Toddlers — Chapter 4
Suggested Responses to Workbook Assignments

Her Imagination Soars

Student Objectives

1. To give three examples of the toddler's intense desire to mimic and to "help" her parent.

2. To list three techniques for helping a toddler learn to talk.

Please read pages 56-65. Answer these questions.

1. Why is music important for toddlers? What does it have to do with brain development?
   Music stimulates brain development because the child hears it, moves with it, and may sing with it.

2. List at least five ways a toddler can "help."
   Personal response but may include such things as bringing diaper to mom, helping her wash the dishes, mop the floor, etc.

3. What should you do if your toddler uses a "bad" word? Should you punish her? Why or why not?
   Don't punish her. Ignore her comment. She doesn't know what the word means, and giving her attention for saying it is likely to encourage her to repeat the word.

4. Other than talking with and reading to your child, what can you do to help him learn to talk? List two things.
   1. Speak clearly to him but don't correct his speech.
   2. Give him reasons to talk. Don't instantly give him something simply because he points at it. Ask him what he wants.

5. What kind of books is your toddler most likely to enjoy?
   Books with bright simple pictures, preferably of things and people she already knows about.

6. What is a non-sexist book?
   A non-sexist book is a book that doesn't limit what a person does by his or her sex.

Writing Assignment

Write an essay in which you discuss a child's pretend play. Did you ever have an imaginary friend? If you can remember your own pretend play, share your memories.

Projects

1. Make a "Book of (your child's name) Words." Show it to your teacher and, more important, read it to a child.

2. Read a picture book to a toddler. Report on your experience.

He's bonding with his baby.

4

Equality in Parenting for Moms and Dads

Too often in teen parent programs, the focus is on the mothers, with little attention paid to the fathers. Half the children in the United States spend at least part of their growing-up years with a single parent, and that parent most often is the mother.

If the dad is absent, a child is more likely to use drugs, suffer depression, and have poor school performance and lower self esteem, according to Jon Morris, author of ***ROAD to Fatherhood*** (Morning Glory Press). These children from fatherless homes are at increased risk for living in poverty and committing crimes. If Dad's not there to provide, care for, and discipline, Mom often has a hard time enforcing rules, instilling values, and mentoring her children's lives.

If a boy's father is out of his life completely, where does he

get his role model for how a father should be? Ray is only 15,
but he understands the importance of the dad being involved
with his child:

> *A good dad is someone who takes time out of his life to
> be there, to keep the family together, to be with the mom
> and the baby, to play with them, just be a dad. I'd like to
> be a good dad.*
>
> Ray, 15 (Adonna, 16, six months pregnant)

Single parents can be good parents — whether it's Mom or
Dad raising the child. However, two loving and caring parents
offer obvious benefits for the child, whether or not the parents
are living together. Teen dads like Ray need to learn the art and
skills of parenting, too.

Young Moms Often the Focus

As you teach young people about parenting, are you focusing
mostly on young mothers? Most programs do. For one thing, it's
easier to find the moms. Dad may be at another school, or working during your group sessions or home visits, or perhaps he's
away in the Armed Forces or in jail for a time.

Too often teen fathers are simply pushed out of the picture. It
may be the young mother's parents who insist she have nothing
to do with him, because they consider their daughter's untimely
pregnancy his fault. It may be the teen mom herself who doesn't
want her child's dad around. Feelings toward a partner tend to
change rapidly when you're 15.

Sometimes there are good reasons for non-involvement with
the father. If he's a drug addict, or considers life in his gang
more important than his family, or if he's violent toward her and/
or their child, mother and baby may be better off without him.

Too often, however, people assume a teen dad is a poor influence without good reason to do so. Perhaps he's acting like a
16-year-old — he's not responsible, and he's not contributing
money to the baby's support. Could it be because he's 16?

Or he may not know much about babies and toddlers. This is
where you can help.

A Father's Rights

A father, no matter how young he is, has the right to spend time with his child whether or not he provides financial support — unless the court has decreed otherwise. And, of course, the same is true of the mother if it's Dad who is rearing their child.

Some of the teen fathers I interviewed resent the power which young mothers seem to hold. Social services for teenage parents often discourage the active participation of fathers, making them feel as though they are powerless to obtain visitation without paying child support.

This, along with pressure from the teen mother's family, leads many teenage fathers to drop out of school and get low paying, dead-end jobs without looking at the long-range picture of continued poverty for himself and his family.

When fathers begin to understand their parenting options, they're more likely to tap their personal and community resources to gain skills, earn money, and become positive parents. Their children are less likely to be homeless or dependent on help from social services. Society as a whole is the real winner.

Whether or not the child's parents are together, however, their child needs both of them. Both parents need your services to help them learn the art and skills of parenting.

> *Fathers need to get into classes like this so they can really know about the baby. Some men, when they find out she's pregnant, leave because they don't know nothing about it. If they learn what it's like, they're more likely to stay. This baby will be part of your life until you die, and you need to know what you're doing.*
> Agie, 18 - Mia, 1 month (Shalaine, 18)

Both mother and child need the emotional support dad can provide. He certainly can help with the physical care of his child. Building a strong relationship with both parents is important for the child and for the parents. If they have the chance, many young fathers mature and rise to the responsibility of caring for this new life they helped create. When dad is pushed out, everybody loses.

Ten Commandments
for Working with Teen Dads

1. Assume he is a good person.

2. Search and serve. (Find him!)

3. Start with client's realities.

4. Help him believe he is—or can be—a good parent.

5. Help him understand that parenting begins at conception.

6. Help him understand his rights as a parent. Encourage
   him to stablish paternity.

7. Help him become the expert on his own child.

8. Believe teen fathers and mothers are the best teachers and
   act on that belief.

9. Encourage him to experience the joys of parenting.

10. In-service staff periodically — to all these concepts.

School and Community Can Help

The father's needs are much like the mother's. No longer can
we assume that mom will be home behind the white picket fence
taking care of the kids while Dad earns the living. Both Mom
and Dad are likely to be working, and both need to be involved
in the care and nurturing of the children. Dads need parenting
skills as much as mothers do, just as moms need to be able to do
their share in providing financial support for the family.

When you meet a teen dad, start out by assuming he's a good
person and would like to parent his child well — just as you
do with teen moms. Then help him improve his knowledge and
skills with children.

He will learn best if you focus on the skills he needs for
his child at the child's current age. Like teen moms, teen dads
cognitively can't look very far ahead. Since the first three years
of a person's life are considered the most important, focusing on
those years with your parents almost guarantees you will make a
significant difference in the lives of their children.

While financial support is an important part of parenting,

being a dad involves far more. Being a dad means providing emotional support, physical care, guidance and love to one's child. Whether or not he is married to or even lives with his baby's mother, a young father can provide some of these important ingredients. He needs to maintain as strong a relationship as possible with his child. He has responsibilities, yes, but he also has rights. One of those rights is to love and care for his child. Even if he and the mother are no longer together, his baby needs him.

Even a very young man can provide emotional support and encouragement to his partner throughout pregnancy. He can encourage her to eat the foods she and their baby need and to stay away from alcohol and other drugs, and perhaps model this behavior. Together, they can take prepared childbirth classes, and he can assist her as she labors and delivers their child.

> *She was crabbier during pregnancy. We'd see each other three or four times a week, and we used to get into fights a lot.*
> *The father should just deal with it regardless what mood he's in, just sit there and take it. If she do make you mad, you should walk out and go to the park and relax. Don't turn your back because that puts a big hurt on her.*
> Jermaine, 18 - Amy, 1 year (Angela, 17)

After his baby is born, he can help guide and care for his child providing he is allowed and encouraged to do so. He can experience the joys of parenting even if he doesn't live with his child. Experiencing the joys is a strong step toward handling his parental responsibilities.

Learning Gentle Techniques
for Disciplining (Teaching) Toddler

Some teen fathers may not realize the wisdom of gentle teaching of babies and toddlers rather than utilizing harsh discipline. They may not understand that hitting little people mostly teaches them that bigger people can hit smaller persons, and that spanking is not a good strategy for encouraging behavior change.

Alton expresses this concept well:

> *Spanking is not teaching them to stop. Hitting on them just makes them mad, and they do it again. But teaching, you show them they're not supposed to mess with it. As they grow older, they'll know that's wrong.*
>
> *When my family spanked me, I knew what I did was wrong—but it made me angrier and angrier, and I'd keep on doing it. I'd rob and everything, and they kept locking me up. Now that I have kids, I know there's no use treating them as I was treated.*

> Alton, 17 - Britney and Jakela, 1 year (Sharrell, 19)

See chapter 6 for more discussion of disciplining babies and toddlers.

Finding the Fathers

Sometimes, to find the dads, all you need to do is ask. A few years ago Julie Vetica, teacher in a teen mother program in Norwalk, California, decided to try out a two-week curriculum for teen dads which she had developed in graduate school. Her school was small, about 250 students. She discussed her plan not only with her principal and other staff members, but also with the students.

Within a week Julie had fourteen teen fathers signed up for her special curriculum. Most amazing was the fact that none of these young fathers was the partner or former partner of any of the teen moms in Julie's class, and none had fathered a baby that was enrolled in the school's infant center. As Julie said, "This isn't Noah's Ark. They don't always come two by two."

Whether or not you're working within a school, do everything you can to let your community know about the program you're offering or plan to offer for teenage fathers.

Publicize your class, your program. Send press releases regularly to local papers. Suggest feature stories with a positive slant about your clients (with their permission, of course).

Make sure counselors, teachers, social workers, and other concerned persons in your community know about your services. Remind your students frequently that they can help teen parents stay in school by telling them about the parenting class and other special services you offer.

Most teen fathers need and want help with job training, job placement, and financial aid information. Be ready to provide this kind of information and referral as well as help with learning the art and skills of parenting.

Whenever possible, encourage the involvement of the teen father's own parents in the care and parenting of their grand-child. Even if the father shows little interest in his child at first, his parents' continued involvement with the child might lead to change in his behavior later on.

You can help your clients feel that their meeting room is a place where both moms and dads belong. Big posters of young men as well as young women interacting with children in a variety of family situations help create a positive atmosphere. Teen fathers might also share pictures of their babies and other family members.

One corner or bulletin board could illustrate a positive attitude toward employment and the completion of high school.

A male facilitator or co-facilitator is an important part of many successful teen father programs. Some of these young men have never known their father, and a positive male role model is important for them.

For help in developing a program for young fathers, see *ROAD to Fatherhood: How to Help Young Dads Become Loving and Responsible Parents* by Jon Morris (Morning Glory Press). Morris directs a program for young fathers in Roanoke, Virginia. His book provides valuable guidelines, tips and strategies for developing and running a program for young fathers.

Rap Sessions Helpful

Teen fathers' personal lives, just as teen mothers', cannot be kept separate from their parenting education. Sharing personal problems and joys can be an important part of a parenting course. Encourage a feeling of rapport, perhaps even something akin to family, among your participants.

If you meet daily, a weekly rap session, facilitated by an

experienced, capable, and caring counselor, can be an important part of a parenting course. If you meet less often, you might plan to use part of each session for "rapping." While problems cannot be scheduled, if participants know there is a designated period specifically for rapping, they may be better able to concentrate on parenting topics during the remaining sessions.

Even if you're working strictly with independent study students on a one-to-one basis, perhaps you can set up once-a-week group sessions with your pregnant and parenting clients, both fathers and mothers. Sharing their concerns with each other can be extremely helpful to teen dads and moms.

Both planning and flexibility are important when you're leading a counseling group. While it's essential in such a group to focus on the current needs of participants, each session needs to be planned. Planned activities may be as simple as asking each parent to complete two sentences: "Today I feel good about . . ." and "Today I feel bad about . . . " This is likely to get the sharing started.

Another day you might use "The best thing about being a dad is . . ." and "The worst thing about being a dad is . . ."

Two important rules for group discussion of personal issues:
• No one needs to talk if s/he doesn't want to.
• Nothing said in group is repeated to others outside the group.

Special Resources for Teen Dads

Teen fathers are likely to appreciate the picture books, *Do I Have a Daddy? A Story for a Single-Parent Child* by Lindsay and *Goodnight, Daddy* by Angela Seward. A short study guide is available at no extra cost from Morning Glory Press for each of these books.

Too Soon for Jeff by Marilyn Reynolds is a novel about a reluctant teen dad, and will appeal especially to young fathers.

Teen Dads: Rights, Responsibilities and Joys (Lindsay) provides guidance for the all-important job of parenting children from conception to age three. The book is written directly to young fathers. Sprinkled throughout each chapter are direct quotes from young fathers, some of whom live with their children, others who don't.

Teen Dads is based on interviews with 60 teenage fathers, some from the inner city and some from rural areas, some high-achievers who both work and continue their education, and others who, at the time of interview, were in jail. The interviewees represent a wide range of socio-economic and ethnic backgrounds.

These young fathers are struggling with the many issues of parenting-too-soon, and they share the wisdom they have gained as they parent. The book is written at a sixth grade reading level. It is generously illustrated with photographs of teen fathers.

Without exception, these young men want to parent their child, and they want to be good dads. Over and over I heard, "I didn't have a father when I was growing up, and I know what that's like. I don't want that for my child."

Teen Dads, as the title says, covers not just the rights and responsibilities of teenage fathers. The joys are also included, a very important part of parenting.

For many of these young fathers, "responsible parenting" will be difficult, and they need support services.

When Baby Is Crawling

The realities of parenthood hit some young dads when their baby starts crawling. That cute infant is suddenly getting into everything and exhibiting a mind of his own. Many parents experience stress at this time.

For examples of activities concerning babies at the crawling stage, see pages 114-125. These activity pages are reprinted from the *Teen Dads Comprehensive Curriculum Notebook,* and are designed to accompany chapter 7, "When He's Crawling — Watch Out!" in *Teen Dads.*

Many of the 22 suggestions are appropriate for home visits and independent study teaching as well as classroom and other group sessions. See p. 118 for suggested independent study assignments.

Classroom Teaching

Preparing lesson plans for teaching about crawling babies, their developmental stage, their care, and how to deal with and foster their wonderful curiosity can be a fun challenge. Of course you will encourage the dads and moms in your class to share anecdotes of life with a crawler.

See the description of 22 activities on pages 115-117. It is unlikely that you need or want 22 activities for your teaching about crawling babies, but these ideas give you lots of choices. You might organize a week as follows:

Monday. Ask students to share anecdotes of active baby getting into everything, and how families respond (activity #2). Also talk about the importance of baby being able to satisfy his curiosity, and how this affects his learning ability.

Divide the chapter into sections. Ask each student or pair of students to read a specific section and develop responses to the workbook questions over that section.

Tuesday. Discuss the chapter by asking students to respond to their sections of the workbook assignments. Then show the DVD, "She's Much More Active" (activity #7), and discuss.

Wednesday. Include two or three babies aged two to twelve months in this session (activity #1). Discuss characteristics of this stage, while visiting babies model the points you're making.

Or — Have a guest speaker, either a dentist to discuss dental health for babies or an infant center teacher to talk about safety for babies and toddlers. Whether or not you invite a dentist to class, talk about the Nursing Bottle Syndrome. Ask for volunteers to visit a children's dentist's waiting room for an hour or two and observe the children needing dental work (activity #6). Any evidence of Nursing Bottle Syndrome?

Thursday. Ask students to observe their children, then complete the Highlights of Parenting chart (activity #8, p. 121). Disuss, allowing time for each dad to report on his child.

Brainstorm ways to play with child under one year of age (activity #12). Provide safety pointers as needed.

If time allows, show the DVD, "He's Crawling — Help!"

(activity #13).

Friday. Ask students to take quiz over chapters 6 and 7 (p. 124). Have puzzle (p. 120) ready for those who finish in time.

Check all the activities described for this topic. You may find others that would fit your students' needs better than the above.

Group Activities

If you are leading a group or teaching a parenting class, you might invite a children's dentist to talk about care of the baby's first teeth and of the risk of Nursing Bottle Syndrome.

An infant center teacher might discuss toy safety with your group. As a follow-up, provide a variety of toys to be evaluated using the "Rating a Toy" handout on p. 122. This activity is also feasible if you work with young parents individually.

Can you have two or three crawling babies in class to help demonstrate this stage? If you are a home visitor, is there a baby there who will "demonstrate"?

A puzzle is included. If you work with a group, they might like to work the puzzle in pairs rather than individually.

Two DVDs are suggested, Your Baby's First Year Series, Volume 2, "She's Much More Active (4-8 months)," and Discipline from Birth to Three Series, Volume 2, "He's Crawling — Help! (6-12 months)" (Morning Glory Press). You might like to show one of these at one session, the other the next time you meet.

Check the other activities. Brainstorming is a good teaching technique, so notice activities #12 and #13.

Teaching Individuals

The activities included for discussion, writing, and brainstorming can, of course, be useful whether you teach groups or individuals. As mentioned before, if no school credit is involved, your clients may prefer to discuss rather than write the assignments. Or perhaps you are encouraging them to keep a journal whether or not it's a school requirement.

When you include both fathers and mothers in your teaching, everybody wins.

Topic: Crawling Baby
Teen Dads: Rights, Responsibilities and Joys

Chapter 7

When He's Crawling — Watch Out! — pp. 84-95

Objectives: Student will be able to

1. Discuss the continuing importance of responding to baby's needs.

2. List three toys which would be enjoyed by a child aged 6-12 months.

3. Describe Nursing Bottle Syndrome and how to prevent it.

4. Describe the importance of talking and playing with the baby.

5. Describe various ways to play with a baby.

SUPPLEMENTARY RESOURCES

Demonstration. Babies aged two to twelve months to illustrate stages of development during this time.

Video. Your Baby's First Year Series, Volume 2, "She's Much More Active (4-8 months)." (Morning Glory Press)

Speaker. Children's dentist.

Speaker. An infant center teacher to discuss toy safety.

Teen Dads **Workbook,** pp. 13-14.

Toys for "Rating a Toy" activity.

Video. Discipline from Birth to Three Series, Volume 2, "He's Crawling — Help! (6-12 months)." (Morning Glory Press)

Picture Books for class project.

TEACHER PREPARATION — CHAPTER 7

1. **Review Chapter 7**, text, pp. 84-95, and the workbook assignments and suggested responses, p. 86 of this *Notebook*. Review the quiz over chapters 6 and 7, p. 85. Quiz key is on p. 86.

2. **Review the learning activities**, decide which ones you will use, and reproduce the needed hand-outs for students. Suggested for this chapter are: "Watch Out, He's Crawling," p. 79; "It's a Secret" puzzle, p. 80; "Highlights of Parenting" chart, p. 81; "Rating a Toy," p. 82; "Picture Book Report," p. 83; and quiz over chapters 6 and 7, p. 85.

3. **Prepare for a demonstration** of babies aged 2-12 months to illustrate developmental stages.

4. **Schedule a children's dentist and/or an infant center teacher** to talk with your group.

5. **Have the videos available,** "She's Much More Active" from Your Baby's First Year Series and "He's Crawling — Help!" from the Discipline from Birth to Three Series (Morning Glory Press). Review and check video teacher's guides for teaching suggestions.

6. **Arrange to have a variety of toys** available for the "Rating a Toy" activity.

7. **Bring picture books** to class for Enrichment Activity #1.

.

CORE CURRICULUM — GROUP LEARNING

Reading Assignment (individually or together)
Chapter 7, *Teen Dads: Rights, Responsibilities and Joys,* "When He's Crawling — Watch Out!" pp. 84-95. **Discuss.** Workbook questions (pp. 13-14) can guide discussion. See p. 86 for suggested responses to workbook assignments.

LEARNING ACTIVITIES — CHAPTER 7

1. **Demonstration.** Babies aged two to twelve months to illustrate stages of development during this time. Discuss characteristics of this stage, and let visiting babies model the points you're making.

2. **Discussion.** Share anecdotes of active baby getting into everything, and how families respond. Discuss positive ways to discipline (teach) child at this stage — child-proofing, substitute item, etc.

3. **Discussion.** Importance of baby being able to satisfy his curiosity, and how this affects future learning ability. Then **brainstorm** examples of baby showing curiosity.

Learning activities continued on next page

LEARNING ACTIVITIES — CHAPTER 7 — CONT.

4. **Writing Assignment** (Workbook). Ask each participant to pretend he is a bright, curious toddler. His dad or mom puts him in a playpen every day for an hour or two. How does he feel about it? Tell each one to write a paragraph describing his feelings, using lots of adjectives.

5. **Puzzle.** "It's a Secret," p. 80. Ask students to complete the puzzle, individually or in pairs, then discuss the concepts illustrated.

6. **Discussion.** Nursing Bottle Syndrome. Ask for volunteers to visit a children's dentist's waiting room for an hour or two and observe the children needing dental work. Any evidence of Nursing Bottle Syndrome?

7. **Video.** Show and discuss Your Baby's First Year Series, Volume 2, "She's Much More Active." See teacher's guide accompanying video for discussion help.

8. **Baby Report.** Ask students to observe their children, then complete the "Highlights of Parenting" chart on page 81. Discuss, allowing time for each student to report on his child.

9. **Speaker.** An infant center teacher to discuss toy safety.

10. **Discussion Starter.** "Rating a Toy" sheet, p. 82. Arrange to have toys available for rating. Begin with a discussion of the value to a child of playing, and of the parent providing a few well-designed toys appropriate for the child's stage of development. Discuss the rating guidelines before they actually rate the toys.

11. **Brainstorm.** Ways to play with child under 12 months of age. Provide safety pointers as needed.

12. **Brainstorm.** List of small objects commonly available at home that would be fun and safe for a baby aged 4-8 months. Then, as **homework,** ask each student to put together a container of small items suitable for a 4-8-month-old baby to play with on the floor. Ask them to share the filled containers, or, if this is not feasible, to report on the items they included.

13. **Video.** Show and discuss Discipline from Birth to Three Series, Volume 2, "He's Crawling — Help! (6-12 months)." See teacher's guide accompanying video for discussion help.

14. **Writing Assignment.** Again, ask them to pretend, this time that they are eight months old. Recently he has realized how different mother or dad is from people they seldom see. When grandma came the other day, he was afraid. How did he feel when grandma insisted on grabbing him and holding him? What did he want her to do? Ask each one to write a colorful paragraph describing his feelings.

15. **Writing Assignment** (Workbook). Ask each student to describe in detail how he could childproof his home to make it safe for a crawling baby and to protect his possessions. As preparation, tell them to crawl through their home to observe, at baby's level, the things they need to put away for awhile.

16. **Quiz.** Chapters 6 and 7, p. 85. **Quiz key,** p. 86.

Learning activities continued on next page

FATHER/CHILD ACTIVITIES — CHAPTER 7 — CONT.

17. **Baby Assignment.** Watch your baby for 15 minutes and list all the things the baby is curious about. Put the list in your journal.

18. **Father/Baby Assignment.** After you make a book for your baby (see below), read it to her. Does she like the book?

19. **Father/Baby Assignment.** Play patty-cake and peek-a-boo with your child — or with another child if yours isn't ready for these games. Write a report of your activity.

ENRICHMENT ACTIVITIES

1. **Picture Book Evaluation.** Bring a stack of picture books. Divide students into pairs. Ask each to choose a picture book and read it to his partner. Then discuss why they chose that particular book. See handout for evaluating picture books, p. 83.

2. **Project.** Make a book for a baby. Students can illustrate their books themselves or choose colorful pictures from magazines or other source. Family photos also provide excellent illustrations.

3. **Speaker.** Children's dentist to discuss care of baby's first teeth. Ask the dentist to talk about Nursing Bottle Syndrome and how to prevent it.

INDEPENDENT STUDY ASSIGNMENTS — CHAPTER 7

Topic: Crawling Baby
Teen Dads: Rights, Responsibilities and Joys

Resources:

Text: *Teen Dads* and Workbook, Chapter 7, "When He's Crawling — Watch Out!" pp. 84-95.

Handouts:

"Watch Out, He's Crawling," p. 79.

"It's a Secret" puzzle, p. 80.

"Highlights of Parenting" chart, p. 81.

"Picture Book Report," p. 83.

"Rating a Toy," p. 82.

Quiz over chapters 6 and 7, p. 85.

1. **Read Chapter 7,** *Teen Dads: Rights, Responsibilities and Joys,* "When He's Crawling — Watch Out!" pp. 84-95. Complete assignments in Workbook (pp. 13-14) including writing assignments and the project.

2. **Handout.** Review "Watch Out, He's Crawling," and place in your notebook.

3. Write in your **Journal.** Suggestion: React to the information in the above handout.

4. **Writing Assignment.** Think about the importance of baby being able to satisfy his curiosity, and how this affects future learning ability. Then **brainstorm** examples of baby showing curiosity. List your ideas. Then pretend (Workbook writing assignment #2) you are a bright, curious toddler. Your dad or mom puts you in a playpen every day for an hour or two. How do you feel about it? Write a paragraph describing your feelings. Use lots of adjectives.

5. **Puzzle.** Complete the "It's a Secret" puzzle.

6. **Baby Report.** Carefully observe your child, then complete the "Highlights of Parenting" chart.

7. **Project.** Put together a container of small items suitable for a 4-8-month-old baby to play with on the floor. Show it to your teacher. Most important, offer it to a 4-8-month-old baby. Describe his reactions in your journal.

8. **Writing Assignment.** Describe specific examples of an active baby getting into everything, and how families respond. Discuss in writing positive ways to discipline (teach) child at this stage — child-proofing, substitute item, etc.

9. **Writing Assignment.** Pretend you are eight months old. Recently you have realized how different mother or dad is from people you seldom see. When grandma came the other day, you were afraid. How did you feel when grandma insisted on grabbing you and holding you? What did you want her to do? Write a colorful paragraph describing your feelings.

10. **Choose a toy** you think is appropriate for a child 2-12 months old. Describe and evaluate it, using the "Rating a Toy" sheet.

11. **Quiz.** Take the quiz over chapters 6 and 7.

Reprinted with permission
from ***Teen Dads Comprehensive Curriculum Notebook.***
Reduced to 60%. To reproduce at full size, enlarge to 150%.

Prepared by Deborah Cashen, author of *Creating Parenting Notebooks*

Teen Dads — Chapter 7

Watch Out, He's Crawling

YOUR 5 – 8 MONTH OLD BABY

✓ My toys need to be big enough to hold easily, yet too big to put in my mouth.

✓ My toys should be washable with no sharp edges or corners. Please remove any parts that come off easily.

✓ I want to touch and handle everything possible!

✓ Balls are my favorite toy; I can roll them, crawl after then, and throw them.

✓ I love it when you play with me.

✓ I love to go outdoors with you, but watch me closely.

✓ I'd rather be carried in your arms than be left in an infant seat.

✓ Let me know I can trust you by responding to my cries as promptly as possible.

✓ Always, whatever my age, treat my fears as the reality they are. Please help me deal with my fear, not scold me.

✓ I'm getting clingy and love for you to hold me, especially around strangers.

✓ Talk to me, even though I may only respond by babbling. I'm learning new ways to communicate by listening to you. I love it when you read to me.

✓ **Never leave me unattended. I get into *everything*!**

✓ I may drool more than usual, because I am getting my teeth.

✓ Avoid putting me to bed with a bottle of milk or juice, so my teeth will have an opportunity to grow in healthy. If I insist on a bottle, put water in it.

✓ I like to have time to calm down before being put to bed. When you spend quiet time with me, rocking me or giving me my last bottle for the night, I fall asleep easier.

✓ Don't be surprised if I show signs of a temper or frustration. I could use a little extra cuddling during these bursts of independence.

Teen Dads, Chapter 7 (Edie De Avila)

It's A Secret

This information can't stay secret for long. Your busy toddler just found the ancient code!

Code: A|B|C D|E|F G|H|I ... J|K|L M|N|O P|Q|R ... T S U V ... X W Y Z

Examples: A = ⌐ N = ⊡ T = ∨ Y = ⟨

1. Your baby is _____. He has something special to offer.

2. In her first 9 months, your pre-toddler _____ tremendously.

3. At different rates, pre-toddlers learn to _____, and stand up.

4. Your pre-toddler is curious. He needs to _____ with your close supervision.

5. Now your baby finds that she can _____ things.

Answers: 1 = unique, 2 = changes, 3 = sit, crawl, 4 = explore, 5 = make, happen

Teen Dads, Chapter 7 (Form developed by Bobbi Ackley)

How I Play with My Child	Physical Development	Highlights of Parenting
		Name of Parent _____ Name of Child _____ Age of Child _____ Date _____
Safety Precautions	Mental Development	Sleeping Patterns
Problems and Decisions	Emotional Development	Feeding Patterns
Feelings About Being a Parent	Social Development	Health Concerns

Teen Dads, Chapter 7

Rating a Toy
Form developed by Bobbie Ackley

Description of the toy:

Price: _____   Age range: _____

Rate this toy according to the following:

I. Is this toy—

	Yes/No	Yes because/No because
1. Enjoyable to the child?		
2. Safe (Are there parts that can be swallowed or does it have sharp edges?)		
3. Interesting enough for the child to play with it repeatedly?		
4. Usable in a variety of ways?		
5. The best buy for the money? (How long will it last?)		
6. Appropriate to the child's state of growth and development?		

II. Does this toy—

1. Actually do what it claims to do?		
2. Actively involve the child in using it?		
3. Help provide an understanding of the everyday world?		
4. Challenge, not frustrate the child?		
5. Help the child build a positive self-image?		
6. Suit the child's interests and abilities?		

III. Toys can help children grow in one of the following ways:

Physical Growth: How does this toy help exercise the child's large and small muscles?

Develop physical skills and coordination?

Mental Growth: How does the toy help the child deal with language, numbers, and other kinds of information?

Develop the ability to solve problems?

Creative Growth: How does the toy encourage the child to be imaginative and inventive?

Social Growth: Does the toy give the child practice in getting along with people? How?

Does it help him/her develop communication skills? How?

Teen Dads, Chapter 7

Picture Book Report

Choose a picture book from our library, from home, or the public library. If possible, choose a book appropriate for your child at this time. Before you complete this report, read the book to your child or, if you don't have a child, to another child. If your partner is pregnant, read to your unborn child.

Title of Book _____   **Author** _____

Publisher _____   **Date Published** _____   **Price** _____
1. What is the story about?

2. What is the theme of the book?

3. Does the book have a purpose? If so, what is it?

4. Do the characters appear real to you and your child? Please explain your answer.

5. Does the background or place of the story seem real? Please explain your answer.

6. How can a child become involved in the story and pictures?

7. Do the words and pictures go together? Please explain your answer.

8. Are the pictures and story original and creative? In what ways? If not, please explain.

9. Do **you** like the book? _____ Why or why not?

10. Did your child like the book? _____ (If your child is not yet born, the answer is "Yes"!)

Equality in Parenting for Dads and Moms

Name_____

Teen Dads Quiz — Chapters 6, 7

TRUE/FALSE. Write "T" before the sentence if it is true. Write "F" before it if it is false.

___ 1. If mom is breastfeeding, it's usually best not to give the baby a bottle at all the first couple of weeks.

___ 2. Picking a baby up when she cries is likely to "spoil" her.

___ 3. The more you care for your baby, the faster you will bond with your child.

___ 4. Baby needs to cry in order to exercise her lungs.

___ 5. Feeding baby with a propped bottle is likely to cause an ear infection.

___ 6. Most babies cut their first tooth when they're six or seven months old.

___ 7. Encouraging your baby to drink water helps guard against tooth cavities.

___ 8. Babies usually learn best when they're kept in a playpen several hours each day.

___ 9. Arranging your house so your baby can freely explore will help her learn more about the world around her.

___ 10. Removing him from temptation is the best approach to keeping a ten-month-old out of trouble.

MULTIPLE CHOICE. Circle the letter of *all* correct answers. Some statements have several correct answers.

11. A baby should *never* be fed with a propped bottle because

    a. propped bottles cause ear infections.
    b. he needs the love he gets from being held.
    c. he could choke on milk curd if he spits up.
    d. propping the bottle makes the milk go sour.

12. Playing with your baby includes:

    a. talking to him.
    b. singing to him.
    c. gently moving his legs slowly up and down.
    d. ignoring him.

13. If your friendly baby suddenly seems afraid of strangers at about eight months, he

    a. probably is sick.
    b. has been hurt by a stranger.
    c. has matured enough to know exactly whom he trusts.
    d. is a bad boy.

14. Which of the following groups of toys is most suitable for a one-year-old child?

    a. Rattles, stuffed animals
    b. Tricycles, electric train
    c. Pull toys, big blocks, balls
    d. 10-piece puzzles, marbles

15. When a six- to twelve-month-old baby gets into things he shouldn't touch,

    a. it's because he simply must explore.
    b. he's trying to see what he can get away with.
    c. you should yell at him.
    d. she's being a "bad" child.

SHORT ANSWER

16. Bonding with your baby means _____

_____.

17. If your child wants to take her bottle to bed, the bottle should contain only _____.

18. Reading to your child will help him learn to _____ sooner.

19. The (adult, baby) must take the responsibility for keeping a crawling baby out of trouble.

ESSAY

20-22. Describe "Nursing Bottle Syndrome" — what it is, the effect it may have on a baby, and how to prevent it. Half your grade will depend on the information in your essay, and half will depend on your neatness, grammar, spelling, sentence and paragraph structure.

23-25. Write a paragraph in which you explain the reasons for child-proofing one's home before the baby starts to crawl.

Teen Dads: Rights, Responsibilities and Joys — Chapter 7
Suggested Responses to Workbook Assignments

When He's Crawling — Watch Out!

Student Objectives

1. To list three toys which a child aged 6-12 months would enjoy.

2. To discuss reasons for and how to baby-proof one's home.

3. To describe Nursing Bottle Syndrome and how to prevent it.

Please read pages 84-95, and complete the following assignments:

1. Why are balls such good toys for baby? *She can roll them and throw them. When she starts crawling, she can go after them.*

2. What does playing with dolls do for boys and girls? *Gives them early practice for being parents.*

3. What should you do if your baby is afraid of something? *Help him deal with his fear.*

4. If you don't see your child often, what may happen when he's about eight months old? *He may suddenly feel afraid.* What can you do about this? *Let him come to me on his own terms.*

5. How can you help your baby learn to talk? *Talk to her. Read to her.*

6. What does baby-proofing mean? *Putting up or away the things baby could damage and the things that could hurt baby.*

7. What's wrong with putting baby in a playpen? *He learns more if he crawls freely through his house or apartment.*

8. When does the average baby start teething? *When he's six or seven months old.*

9. Describe two things you could do to help baby if her gums hurt. *1. Give her teething rings to chew on — rings that have been put in the freezer first. 2. Put teething lotion on her gums.*

10. If baby gets a fever of about 101° while he's teething, do you blame it on the teething? Why or why not? *No. A fever indicates an infection and should be treated.*

11. Why should you keep soda, candy, and other sweet foods away from your child? *They aren't good for her teeth.*

12. Describe Nursing Bottle Syndrome. What is it and why does it happen? *Nursing Bottle Syndrome happens when a child takes a bottle of milk to bed with him. The milk pooling in his mouth rots his front teeth.*

13. How can you prevent Nursing Bottle Syndrome if baby wants to take a bottle to bed? *Put water in the bottle.*

14. How can you help your child go to bed without lots of fussing? *Develop a bedtime routine you follow every night.*

15. Describe several ways to play with a year-old child. *Answers could include: Play follow the leader. Play with him outdoors. Other answers are acceptable.*

Writing Assignments

1. Describe in detail how you could child-proof your home to make it safe for a crawling baby and to protect your possessions. As preparation, crawl through your home to observe, at baby's level, the things you need to put away for awhile.

2. Pretend you are a bright, curious toddler. Your dad or mom puts you in a playpen every day for an hour or two. How do you feel about it? Write a paragraph describing your feelings. Use lots of adjectives.

Project

Play patty cake and peek-a-boo with your child — or with another child if yours isn't ready for these games. Write a report of your activity.

Take the quiz over chapters 6 and 7.

Quiz Key — Chapters 6, 7				
1-2-F	6-T	10-T	14-c	18-talk *or* read
3-T	7-T	11-a, b, c	15-a	19-adult
4-F	8-F	12-a, b, c	16-falling in love	20-22-essay
5-T	9-T	13-c	17-water	23-25-paragraph

Cheerios® and milk — so much better for him than French fries.

5

Nutrition – Good Eating for Two Generations

If you could change a young parent's eating habits, where would you start? And would you focus on the parent or the child?

Would you begin with prenatal nutrition? Or would you move immediately to doing what you could to get them weaned away from fast foods, at least to some extent?

Find ways to cut back on obesity? Or suggest how to help a toddler like vegetables?

Starting with Pregnancy

Pregnant teens usually want the best for their unborn baby. We know that feeding the fetus the food it needs is crucial, and that love for the unborn is a convincing incentive.

Find out what your students/clients already know about nutrition. Being well informed about what we should eat doesn't necessarily make us eat as we should. However, if we don't know the difference nutritionally between a French fry and a carrot, and we've been indoctrinated into the French fry culture, we aren't likely to choose the carrot. Start with a quick nutrition pretest. See example below. The information comes straight from **MyPyramid.com** and the book, *Mommy, I'm Hungry! Good Eating for Little Ones* (Lindsay, Brunelli, and McCullough). Results from the quiz can guide you in teaching the importance of each of the food groups to her and to her unborn baby.

Whether or not they are pregnant, offering the pretest, then teaching nutrition basics as needed is a good foundation toward helping them develop better eating habits.

Nutrition Pretest

1. List the five basic food groups and the amount (in cups or ounces) you need to eat from each group each day to remain at your healthiest.

2. If you don't like milk, what can you eat and/or drink to get the calcium you need each day?

3. How many extra calories do you need a day if you're pregnant?

4. Why are fruits and vegetables an important part of your diet?

5. Describe the difference between a portion and a serving of food.

6. Why are french fries not considered a vegetable by some people?

7. Is it possible to order and eat healthy meals at some fast food restaurants?

8. Does overweight have anything to do with becoming diabetic? Why is there such an increase in Type II diabetes among school-age children?

9. List three carbohydrates that are good for you.

10. List three carbohydrates that are bad for your health.

Key: 1. Grains, 6 oz.; vegetables, 2.5 cups; fruits, 2 cups; milk, 3 cups; meat and beans, 5.5 oz. **2.** soy or rice milk, foods containing calcium and those fortified with calcium, vitamin D. **3.** 400. **4.** Contain lots of vitamins and minerals. **5.** Portion is amount eaten while a serving is a specified amount. **6.** Because they're so greasy and salty. **7.** Yes. **8.** Yes. Increase is because so many children are overweight and don't exercise. **9.** Whole grains, fruits, vegetables. **10.** Soda, candy, other high-sugar foods.

Fast Food Reality

Another good way to begin teaching about nutrition is to show the "Super Size Me" DVD, which shows a man living on food from McDonald's® for a month. In the process, his health seriously deteriorates.

Mommy, I'm Hungry! starts with a chapter on prenatal nutrition, continues with one on breastfeeding and one on introducing solid food. We decided the fast food chapter should be next, before even beginning a discussion of food for toddlers.

French fries are one of the three vegetables (if you consider them a vegetable) most eaten by babies nine months old. By the time they are 18 months old, the average baby eats more French fries than any other vegetable. We can help young parents understand they don't need to *teach* their babies and toddlers to eat a food so high in salt and fat. The longer they can wait to introduce these foods, the better for the child. And if this means foregoing French fries themselves, the parents, too, will, of course, be better off.

It won't work, however, to try too hard to talk teens out of eating all fast foods. Unfortunately, fast foods are a way of life for many people in our culture.

A better goal is to encourage students to cut back on the fast foods they eat, and when they go to fast food restaurants, to make healthier choices than a double cheeseburger, large order of fries, and giant soda. See *Mommy, I'm Hungry!* for suggestions for better choices than these typical items. One example:

	Calories	Protein	Carbs	Fat	Sodium
Grilled steak taco fresco style	280	12	21	5	650
Pintos and cheese	180	10	20	7	700
Ice water with fresh lemon	0	0	0	0	0
Totals	**460**	**22**	**41**	**12**	**1350**

Ask for pintos without cheese to lower the fat and sodium in your meal.

(Taco Bell®)

Portions Versus Servings

Portions and servings are often two very different concepts. A pregnant teen needs three servings of protein foods daily, but this doesn't mean she needs a 6-ounce hamburger plus two more servings of protein. The big hamburger is the portion she is served. That 6-ounce portion of meat counts as two servings. If she doesn't like vegetables, so chooses to eat only one spoonful of peas, her portion doesn't make a serving of vegetables. It takes about half a cup of peas to make one serving.

Provide opportunities for your students to read and understand food labels. If she's pregnant, she needs about 2600 calories each day, 50-70 grams of protein, 175 grams of carbohydrate, and 66 grams of fat. If they read food labels or the nutrition charts at fast food restaurants, they have a guide as to whether or not that food is "worth" eating. For more information on reading labels, see pp. 39-41, *Mommy I'm Hungry!*

Breast Is Best for Baby

The American Academy of Pediatrics (AAP) recommends that all infants be breastfed for at least six months, preferably a year. We know that breastfed babies are less likely to get sick, and that they are less likely to have health problems when they are adults. Breastfeeding, once it is established, is also easier for Mom. Yet the majority of teen mothers either breastfeed for a very short time, or not at all.

There are reasons for this seeming aversion to breastfeeding. Perhaps no one in her family has ever breastfed a baby. Perhaps more important, her boyfriend may consider her breasts sexual objects, and says he doesn't want a baby "hanging on them."

Even the hospital may not be supportive. Over and over, I hear of nurses insisting the newborn must have a bottle, surely a great technique for ensuring that the new mom will have more trouble getting her baby to latch on, and may be the reason she switches to bottles.

Encourage her to make a birth plan before she delivers. Include her decision to breastfeed, perhaps in big black (or red) letters. Give the plan to her obstetrician, pediatrician, all nurses she encounters, and anyone else involved with the birth and her aftercare.

Grandparents and the baby's father want the best for this baby, and they may not know the importance of breastfeeding. Educating these important people in her life may help.

Breastfeeding at School

Even if the teen understands the importance of breastfeeding and decides this is how she will feed her infant, and even if her family, boyfriend, and other friends are supportive, she may have other big obstacles.

If she is in school, how can this possibly work? In fact, school may be her biggest obstacle. Yet, continuing her education is all-important, too. How can school be combined with breastfeeding?

First, she needs to stay home with her baby for at least four, and preferably six weeks. It is imperative that she and her baby get a good start with feeding. Most babies need to be fed about every couple of hours during those early days, and Mom needs to rest as much as possible.

If she returns to a school with infant care on campus, breast-feeding is probably quite possible. Can she be called out of class when her baby needs her?

Teen Parent Program teachers who strongly encourage the practice are helping provide a wonderful gift to the babies involved. Other teachers in the school may play a big role in whether students breastfeed their babies. See p. 132 for the note a Teen Parent nurse sends to teachers when a breastfeeding student returns to school. This can help teachers understand the importance of their support.

Another important aspect of successful breastfeeding is the provision of a comfortable place at school for students to feed their babies and breast-pump as needed.

If she can't have her baby at school with her, how can she continue breastfeeding? Some students manage a shorter school schedule during those breastfeeding months. One teen reported that she fed her baby right before she left for school, and that her mother brought the baby to her for feeding during the late

Teens and Breastfeeding in Boulder, CO

Breastfeeding can work for school-age moms.

The Fairview Teen Parent Program, Boulder, CO, has an unusually high percentage of breastfeeding mothers. Almost 100 percent start breastfeeding, according to nurse Leslie Boyhan, and the majority continue. She provided information on the fifteen children currently in the nursery who had been there since infancy:

In the infant section, NS, AM, and JP, mothers of a two-month-old, 2.5 months, and 6 months, are still breastfeeding. NS and IA stopped breastfeeding at 3 and 2 months because moms didn't want to be pulled from class to feed baby. AM also breastfed for three months. KA stopped at 3 weeks. (Her mother and sister did not support breastfeeding.)

Most mothers of crawlers continue breastfeeding, although one, NM, stopped at two weeks. (Mother "did not like it.") NH is still breastfeeding at 10 months, YH at 13 months, and IRC, 8 months. YT breastfed for 7 months. (She said her milk "dried up.") AL did not breastfeed because her preemie stayed in the hospital while Mom worked.

One mother of a toddler breastfed for a year; another for two days because she "did not like breast-feeding."

Other toddlers in the nursery were not there when they were infants, so Boyhan did not include them in her research.

One reason for this impressive record is the letter Boyhan routinely sends to each breastfeeding student's teachers:

To the Teachers of _____,

_____ is returning to school next week after having a beautiful baby girl, Alexis. _____ is breastfeed-ing. Please excuse the disruption if she is pulled from class in order to feed her baby. Generally, the baby will need to feed every 2-4 hours during the first few months after returning to school.

Please contact me with any questions.

Leslie Boyhan, Teen Parent Program Nurse, 303.447.5346

morning break. The teen mom's classes ended at 2 p.m. She said her baby adapted by nursing more often when she was home.

If she can't be with her baby during the school day, she needs to pump her breasts. To do so, she needs the equipment and a hospitable place. Is there an empathetic school nurse who is willing to have a comfortable chair in a private place in her office (not in the bathroom!) for the mom's use when needed? If she can't afford a good breast pump, can she borrow one at the local WIC (Special Supplemental Nutrition Program for Women, Infants and Children) office? Or will a local service organization donate one or more to the school for student moms to use?

Breastfeeding, especially during those first six months, is a great gift for her baby.

Of course if she decides, in spite of all your encouragement, to give her baby formula, respect her choice and be sure she understands the importance of cleanliness and of following formula-mixing instructions exactly. At least as important is to discuss how important it is *always* to hold the baby as she — or someone else — gives him his bottle.

Remind her that baby knows how much formula he needs. When he's full — slowed sucking or he turns away from the bottle — it's time to stop. He does not need to finish his bottle.

Introducing Solid Food

By six months, but generally no sooner, baby needs nutrients not included in breast milk or formula. Things to remember:

- Start with rice cereal because it's least likely to cause an allergic reaction. A teaspoon of cereal mixed with three or four teaspoons of breast milk or formula is enough to start with.
- Always wait several days before introducing another new food so that any allergy to that food can be identified.
- From six to about eight months, baby needs extremely smooth food. From eight or nine months on, grinding or chopping table food works well. Buying expensive jars of food is not necessary during this time.
- Preparing the family's food for the baby (before adding salt and other seasonings) may encourage the family to plan more

healthy meals for everyone.

• If the family has carrots or other vegetable, preparing extra for the baby, then freezing it in ice cube tray portions for future use is a good plan.

• Most important, Mom and Dad decide what and when to feed baby, but *baby* decides whether and how much to eat. This is how she learns to respect her appetite.

Whether you work with a class, group, or with individuals, can you have them prepare simple foods for babies of various ages, perhaps six months (you need a blender), nine months, and a year? They are more likely to prepare food at home rather than resorting to buying the jars of food once they see how simple the preparation is.

And remind them that baby doesn't need to taste French fries! Tasting is how he develops a love of fatty and salty foods.

Does baby refuse certain foods? Does he love sweet potatoes but spits smashed peas out? Help your students understand why they need not assume he will never eat peas. Every few weeks, offer peas again, without making a fuss about it. Try at least nine or ten times before giving up on peas (or other disliked food).

Baby's taste buds change as she grows older. What she didn't like at seven months may taste delicious six months later. It's important that she enjoy a variety of foods.

Feeding Picky Toddlers

Toddlers are often categorized as picky eaters, probably for two major reasons. First, they don't need as much food as they did during their first twelve months, and parents often tend to offer even more food now that he's bigger. Second, the toddler has learned he has a mind of his own and he wants to make his own decisions. If Dad wants him to eat what to the baby are huge portions, baby may assert himself by refusing to eat at all.

Toddlers want to make their own decisions. She wants to decide how much and when she eats. Letting her make some of those decisions is important. If she's offered only healthy foods, she is likely to make good choices.

Continue to offer food he has refused in the past, but only one of these foods at a time. The parent needs to be very matter-of-fact about the child's eating. Insisting he eat specific foods won't work very well.

The parent needs to provide several appetizing fruits and vegetables, protein food, and whole grains in addition to milk each day. Keeping a record for a few days of the foods the toddler actually eats and drinks can help a parent figure out whether their picky eater has an eating problem or not. If, over several days, he's getting fruits, vegetables, whole grains, protein, and milk, he's probably doing just fine.

Shopping for Food

Healthy, nutritious food can be expensive. Preparing food at home takes time. It's easy to understand why teens think going to a fast food place is great for many of their meals. Eating out, however, is also expensive, even at fast food places.

> *When I lived with my mom before my pregnancy, my mom cooked and we didn't eat out a lot. When I moved out I was lazy. It was easier to get a pizza or go to McDonald's®. But when you think about it, you can buy a week's groceries for about the price of a visit to McDonald's®.*
> Ukari, 19 – Kendall, 3

Serving TV dinners and other already-prepared foods at home almost always provides less food, and certainly less nutritious dishes, for your money than do foods you make "from scratch."

Time and money spent on groceries and preparing and cooking one's own food is well spent. We can fix a more nutritious and appetizing meal. It may not even take more time if we add up the time spent traveling to and from the restaurant, ordering food, and waiting to be served.

Teen parents who live with their parents may not have much choice in foods that are purchased. Perhaps if they offer to help more with the meal planning, shopping, and food preparation, they can influence their child's food choices as well as their own.

Teen parents tend to be very busy most days. Assign meal planning activities with the proviso that the menus must not

only be nutritious, but also quick and easy to prepare, and that
the ingredients not be overly expensive. Is it possible for them
to prepare food in your classroom or meeting place? Will your
independent study students or home visit clients do some
practice cooking?

Many young people have cooked very little and need to learn
how to prepare simple meals. Note: The *Mommy, I'm Hungry!*
text includes a few recipes, and each chapter of the *Comprehensive Curriculum Guide* for this book has suggestions/recipes for
cooking with children.

Cooking can provide great parent/child togetherness. Even a
toddler can help mom or dad in the kitchen. For instance, he can
wash the lettuce and the fruit. Your group might brainstorm all
sorts of ways their children can help with the cooking.

Of course you'll also discuss safety. Children under three
generally should not cook anything hot. They can help prepare/
measure the ingredients.

Helping Mom or Dad plan meals and shop is likely to result
in a toddler who is willing to eat many of the foods prepared. As
a starter, suggest this bean dip:

Bean Dip

1/3 cup canned refried beans   Grated cheddar cheese
Chips or crackers

Get out a shallow bowl. Place approximately 1/3 cup
canned refried beans in the bowl. Use a fork to flatten beans
along bottom of bowl. If playing is more important than
hunger, this may take a while.

Sprinkle with grated cheddar cheese. Microwave on high
for 45 seconds. Remove, place a circle of chips or crackers
around the edge in the dip to make it look like a flower.

You may have students who either are from vegetarian families or have decided themselves not to eat meat. Vegetarianism
can be a healthy way to go, even during pregnancy, breastfeeding, and for small children. To be healthy, however, means the
parents' and the child's diet *must* be well balanced. It's even

more important that vegetarians eat a wide variety of food including greens, fruits and vegetables, beans, nuts or seeds, eggs and dairy products (unless they're vegan), and a little fat.

Go to the website **<www.mypyramid.gov>** where you can find "Tips and Resources for Vegetarian Diets."

Classroom Teaching

Reproduced here from the *Mommy, I'm Hungry! Comprehensive Curriculum Notebook* are the activities for chapter 4, "Fast Foods and Healthy Eating." Suggested guests include a medical doctor to discuss the effects on health of eating fast foods. S/he needs to focus on children and teens, and be as realistic and believable as possible. Ideal would be a stand-up comic who knows a lot about fast foods.

Also suggested is inviting two or three teens who were eating lots of fast foods, but have cut back a great deal. How did they manage to eat less of these foods?

All of the activities are appropriate for classroom use.

Monday. Perhaps you will start by showing the DVD, "Super Size Me" (activity #8). It offers a look at the damage too much fast food can do. (The actor decided to eat all meals at McDonald's® for 30 days — with dire consequences to his health.)

Ask students to pick up the nutrition handouts that are supposed to be available at fast food restaurants. If they don't find the handouts there, tell them to go to the restaurant's website for this information.

For classroom teaching, you will probably ask at least some of your students to read the chapter and complete the assignments in the workbook. Suggested responses to these assignments are on p. 156.

Tuesday. Tell students to choose their favorite fast food menu, then figure out the calories, carbohydrates, protein, sodium, and fat contained in each item. Then compare this information with the daily recommendations for each nutrient (activity #2, p. 147).

Next, ask them to select a healthier choice from the fast food menus. How do these menus compare with their first choices? As a class, brainstorm at least five typical fast food meals (activity #4). Then figure what to do easily to create a nutritious meal for a toddler who is eating with his parents. Can they find suitable foods on the fast food menu? What take-along food needs to be added? Discuss which restaurants are now offering better choices for toddlers as well as adults.

Or

Using your fast food nutrition chart, tell them to plan three fast food meals for the parent and two for the child, with each meal being fairly nutritious (activity #5, p. 149). Also give them a copy of p. 148, "Facts to Remember."

Wednesday. Discussion questions are provided for two case studies in the text (activity #7, p. 151). In one, a young mom talks about the obesity problem and suggests this happens "because we're lazy." When she works all day, she doesn't want to cook when she gets home. Discussion questions include describing a meal one could fix at home in 15 minutes, a meal more nutritious for a child than a hamburger, French fries, and soda.

In the other case study, Paige describes herself as a former fast food junkie. She then shares the strategies she used to change her eating habits. Do students think any of these ideas might help them change their choices of food?

Thursday. A brief Reader's Theater (activity #11, p. 153) portrays a teen couple who are afraid they are on the way to becoming heavier than they want to be. They decide to cook at home that night. Recipes are given for turkey burgers, baked French fries, and garlic salad (p.154). Can your students prepare this meal at school or as a homework assignment?

If they can prepare it at school but you don't have room to give everyone an opportunity to cook at once, perhaps you could have half the class prepare the meal one day, while the other half works the puzzles (pp. 150 and 152).

Another workbook writing assignment also good for class discussion is activity #12. As preparation, the student counts the number of fast food restaurants within two miles of school or home, then discusses the effect these restaurants have on teens living in the area.

Friday. Assign the suggested parent/child assignment (#14) for the weekend. The parent is to go on a picnic with the child with a lunch they pack together. The picnic might be at a park, in the student's back yard, or in a "tent" made by throwing a blanket over a card or other table.

Ask students to take the quiz over chapters 3 and 4. Note that the quiz and Wordfind puzzle keys are on p. 157.

Also note the two enrichment activities described on p. 143. The first one suggests that students research the number of times class members eat fast food in a week, then figure the range and average number per teen.

The other project, suggested as a writing assignment, would also work well simply as a class discussion. Assume they are concerned about a three-year-old who eats fast food meals nearly every day, but now his parent has decided this is not good for him.

As a class, develop a plan for weaning him away from fast foods. It will be hard for the child, and you don't want to make him completely miserable in the process. Perhaps you will start by brainstorming possible strategies.

Independent Study Assignments

The Independent Study assignments on pp. 144-145 include activities appropriate for independent learning for school credit. As mentioned before, you can simply duplicate the page and the relevant activities for your student. You may decide to delete some activities for some students.

Not-for-Credit Group Activities

About everything mentioned above is appropriate for a group outside the classroom. You probably are not using the workbook except as a discussion guide, and you would ignore the quiz.

Choosing from the other activities, you can create a fun-filled, enjoyable learning session with young parents. And you may make a difference in how they eat and how their children eat.

Home Visit Teaching

You'll find many of these activities are also good for one-on-one teaching. Ascertain first how involved your client is with fast food consumption. How many times has she eaten at a fast food restaurant during the last week? Can you start by showing the "Super Size Me" DVD?

Perhaps you will bring nutrition charts from a couple of fast food restaurants and go over some of the information with your client. Talk about better choices than a super size hamburger, French fries and soda.

Offer her the two puzzles, which she might enjoy completing and will learn more about nutrition in the process.

Suggest the parent/child picnic activity.

Will she prepare the turkey burger/baked French fries/garlic salad meal (p. 154)?

The Obesity Epidemic

"Fat-Proofing Your Child" is chapter 7 in *Mommy, I'm Hungry!* In the *Comprehensive Curriculum Notebook* you will find a lot more teaching activities designed for use with this chapter.

The obesity rate for adults and children in the United States is climbing alarmingly. Appearance is not the biggest problem. A child who is overweight may get teased because of his weight. He may have other emotional and physical problems such as asthma or childhood diabetes. A child who is overweight is more likely to become an obese adult with more health problems.

Help your clients understand the risks of obesity. Discuss strategies to prevent overweight in their child and themselves. Stress the importance of active exercise as well as healthy eating. Help them understand the difference between good and bad carbohydrates and ways to reduce the amount of sugar they consume.

Whatever you do to help young parents and their children eat more healthfully will have an effect on their health in future years as well as now.

Topic: Fast Foods
Mommy, I'm Hungry
Chapter 4

Fast Foods and Healthy Eating — pp. 78-91

Objectives: Student will be able to

1. Describe three fast food meals that are fairly nutritious.
2. Discuss strategies for cutting back on one's consumption of fast foods.
3. Explain the risks of eating too much salt.

SUPPLEMENTARY RESOURCES

Video: "Super Size Me." Available from <www.Amazon.com> $10.

Guest Speaker. Medical doctor.

Special Guests. Find two or three teens who were eating lots of fast food, but have cut back a great deal.

TEACHER PREPARATION — CHAPTER 4

1. **Review Chapter 4,** text, pp. 78-91, and the workbook assignments and suggested responses, p. 85 of this *Notebook.* Also see quiz, p. 84, quiz answer key, p. 86, and Fast Foods puzzle key, p. 86.

2. **Review the learning activities,** decide which ones you will use, and reproduce the needed handouts for students. Suggested for this chapter are: "Fast Foods and Healthy Eating," p. 75; "Favorite Fast Foods," p. 76; "Facts to Remember," p. 77; "Fast Food Project," p. 78; "Fast Foods and Healthy Eating" puzzle, p. 79; "Mini Case Studies," p. 80; "Nutrient Jigsaw Puzzle — Good Fats, Bad Fats," p. 81 (on light cardboard); Reader Theater, "Let's Cook Tonight," p. 82; (Discussion questions for "Let's Cook Tonight," for Independent Study students, p. 86); "Recipes," p. 83; Quiz, p. 84. **Write the journal suggestion and Parent/Child Assignment on the board.**

3. **Note:** It might be convenient to reproduce all the nutrient jigsaw puzzles now because you will need light cardboard for each one. Other jigsaw puzzles, pp. 100, 113, 131, 143, 156, 157, 171.

4. **Obtain and review** the video, "Super Size Me." See Writing Assignment, #7, p. 71. **Note:** This is a long video (90 minutes), and may contain brief sections you would prefer not to show in the classroom, i.e., stomach reduction surgery. The note with the video said a "family version" is to be available soon.

5. **Guest Speaker. Schedule a medical doctor** to discuss the effects on health of eating fast foods. Ask him to focus on children and teens, and to be as realistic as possible.

6. **Special Guests.** Ask two or three teens who were eating lots of fast food why they have cut back a great deal on such food.

7. **Food Preparation.** Have ingredients and equipment ready to prepare recipes, p. 83, for Cajun "Fries," Turkey Burgers, and Jeanne's Salad.

Mommy, I'm Hungry! Comprehensive Curriculum Notebook   70

CORE CURRICULUM — GROUP LEARNING

Reading Assignment (individually or together)
Chapter 4, *Mommy, I'm Hungry!* "Fast Foods and Healthy Eating," pp. 78-91. **Discuss.** Workbook questions (pp. 15-17) can guide discussion. **Optional:** Students write individual or group responses to questions. See p. 85 for suggested responses to workbook assignments.

LEARNING ACTIVITIES — CHAPTER 4

1. **Chapter Summary.** Give each student "Fast Foods and Healthy Eating," p. 75. Discuss.

2. **Favorite Fast Foods.** Ask students to bring in a nutrition brochure from their favorite fast food restaurant. (The information is also available on the restaurant's own website, or a website such as the USDA or http://www.fatcalories.com/. Many health care providers have a booklet listing the most popular foods.) Give each a copy of "Favorite Fast Foods," p. 76, and ask them to follow the directions. Discuss in class. *(Activity from Diane Smallwood)*

3. **Guest Speaker. Medical doctor** to discuss the effects on health of eating fast foods. Ask him to focus on children and teens, and to be as realistic as possible.

4. **Brainstorm.** As a class, list at least five typical fast food meals. Then figure what to do easily to create a nutritious meal for a toddler. Start with anything suitable from the fast-food menu and add take-along food as needed.

5. **Fast Food Project.** (Workbook) Obtain a nutrition chart from your favorite fast food restaurant. Now plan three fast food meals for you and two for your child that are fairly good for you and your child. Figure out the amount of fat, protein, carbohydrates, salt, and calories in each meal. Follow the way the meals were analyzed in this chapter. Do not use the same menus as those in the book. See chart, "Fast Food Project," on p. 78. Also see "Facts to Remember," p. 77.

6. **Wordfind Puzzle.** "Fast Foods and Healthy Eating," p. 79. Ask students to work the puzzle either individually or in pairs. Note: Key is on p. 86.

7. **Case Studies.** Ask students to read these case studies aloud: Caimile, p. 79, and Paige, pp. 90-91, text. Discuss. See discussion questions on p. 80 of this *Notebook*.

8. **Video/DVD: "Super Size Me."** Watch film and discuss. Have students also express their personal reactions to the film in an essay.

9. **Nutrient Jigsaw Puzzle — Good Fats, Bad Fats.** There will be a total of fifteen different nutrient puzzles spaced out over the next seven chapters. Give each student an envelope big enough to hold puzzle pieces without folding. Designate a place to keep the envelopes at school, preferably filed conveniently in alphabetical order. See more detailed instructions on student handout, p. 81.

10. **Special Guests.** Ask two or three teens who were eating lots of fast food why they have cut back a great deal on such food. Ask them to talk about money saved, how they feel physically, etc.

Cont. on next page.

Learning Activities — Cont.

11. Reader Theater. Give two students copies of "Let's Cook Tonight," pp. 82, and ask each one to play one of the roles. Give them time to rehearse, then perform the play for the class. See discussion questions on p. 86.

12. Writing Assignment. (Workbook) Count the number of fast food restaurants within two miles of your home and/or your school. Then write an essay in which you discuss the effect these fast food restaurants have on the teens who live in your area.

13. Journal. Suggested starter: "My favorite fast food meal is . . ."

14. Parent/Child Assignment. Go on a picnic with your child. Pack a lunch for each of you. The picnic might be in a park, your back yard, or in a "tent" in the house (blanket thrown over a card table or other table).

15. Food Preparation. See p. 83. Let students try the baked french fries, turkey burger, garlic salad.

15. Quiz. Ask students to take the quiz for chapters 3 and 4, p. 84. Quiz key, p. 86.Follow the way the meals were analyzed in this chapter. Do not use the same menus as those in the book. See chart,

---

ENRICHMENT ACTIVITIES

1. Research. Ask each student to ask ten teens to tell them the number of times they have eaten fast food in the past week, and to keep a tally of the responses. Add up the total fast food meals eaten by all these teens in a week. What was the average number per teen? The range?

2. Writing Assignment. Assume you have a three-year-old child. You have been taking him out for at least one fast food meal several times a week. But now you have decided this is not good for him. Develop a plan for weaning him away from fast foods. You know it will be hard for your child, and you don't want to make him completely miserable. So what will you do?

INDEPENDENT STUDY ASSIGNMENTS — CHAPTER 4

Topic: Fast Food
Mommy, I'm Hungry!

Resources
Text: *Mommy, I'm Hungry!* and Workbook, Chapter 4.

Handouts

"Fast Foods and Healthy Eating," p. 75

"Favorite Fast Foods," p. 76

"Facts to Remember," p. 77

"Fast Food Project," p. 78

Fast Foods and Healthy Eating puzzle, p. 79

"Mini Case Studies," p. 80

Reader Theater: "Let's Cook Tonight," p. 82

"Recipes— Let's Cook Tonight" p. 83

Quiz, p. 84

Questions, "Let's Cook Tonight," p. 86

Nutrient Jigsaw puzzle — Good Fats, Bad Fats, p. 81

Assignments

1. Read chapter 4, *Mommy, I'm Hungry,* and respond to all questions including the writing assignment and project in your workbook.

2. Chapter Summary. Read "Fast Foods and Healthy Eating," then put in your nutrition notebook.

3. Favorite Fast Foods. Obtain a nutrient listing from your favorite fast food restaurant. (The information is also available on the restaurant's own website, or a website such as the USDA or http://www.fatcalories.com/. Many health care providers have a booklet listing the most popular foods.) Follow the directions on the attached "Favorite Fast Foods."

4. Puzzle. Work the puzzle, "Fast Foods and Healthy Eating."

5. Case Studies. Read these mini case studies: Caimile, p. 79, and Paige, pp. 90-91, text. Respond to the attached discussion questions in writing.

6. Video/DVD: "Supersize Me." Watch the film and express your reactions in an essay.

7. Nutrient Jigsaw Puzzle — Good Fats, Bad Fats. There will be a total of fifteen different nutrient puzzles spaced out over the next seven chapters. Attached is an envelope big enough to hold your puzzle pieces without folding. Each week, place your new nutrient jigsaw puzzle pieces in the envelope with the others. See more detailed instructions on attached handout.

8. Reader Theater. Read "Let's Cook Tonight," and answer the discussion questions in writing.

9. Journal. Suggested starter: "My favorite fast food meal is . . ."

10. Parent/Child Assignment. Go on a picnic with your child. Pack a lunch for each of you. The picnic might be in a park, your back yard, or in a "tent" in the house (blanket thrown over a card table or other table).

Cont. on next page.

Mommy, I'm Hungry! **Chapter 4**
Independent Study Activities — Cont.

11. **Food Preparation.** Prepare the healthy version of a fast food meal. See attached recipes for burgers, french "fries," and salad.

12. **Quiz.** Please take the quiz for chapters 3 and 4.

ENRICHMENT ACTIVITIES

1. **Research.** Ask ten teens to tell you the number of times they have eaten fast food in the past week. Tally the responses. Add up the total fast food meals eaten by these teens in a week. What was the average number per student? The range? (Range is the highest and lowest number.)

2. **Writing Assignment.** Assume you have a three-year-old child. You have been taking him out for at least one fast food meal several times a week. But now you have decided this is not good for him. Develop a plan for weaning him away from fast foods. You know it will be hard for your child, and you don't want to make him completely miserable. So what will you do?

Fast Foods and Healthy Eating

FAST FOODS ARE *EVERYWHERE!*

Problems with Fast Foods

- Far too high in fat.
- Far too high in salt.
- High in carbohydrates.
- May contain more protein than needed.
- Usually extremely high in calories.
- Most calories for children need to come from fruits, vegetables, grains, milk, and protein foods.
- Need to limit the amount of salt in your child's diet — and in yours.
- Need to limit fat in each total meal to 30 percent or less.
- Typical fast food meal (double burger with bacon and cheese, large order of fries, and giant soda) contains 2/3 of a teen's daily calorie needs, 1 1/2 times as much carbohydrate, and more protein, fat, and sodium than needed for the *entire* day.
- Missing in that typical fast food meal — fruits, vegetables, milk, not enough grains.

Better Choices

- Grilled steak taco, pintos and cheese (Taco Bell®).
- Grilled chicken breast without skin, garden salad, 2 corn tortillas (El Pollo Loco®).
- Chicken McNuggets (6), side salad with vinaigrette dressing, low fat milk (McDonalds®).

Absolutely *Not* Recommended

- Any meal with more than 30 percent fat content.
- All fried or "crispy" meats or burritos.
- "Double" or "triple" sandwiches.
- Salads with crispy meats or regular salad dressings.
- Most breakfast choices that include meat or eggs are about 50 percent fat.

If you decide to cut back on fast food, you'll be doing yourself and your child a favor.
It's a big challenge with a huge payoff in better health for both of you.

Mommy, I'm Hungry! **Chapter 4** — Activity from Diane Smallwood

Burgers Tacos Fries Soda

Favorite Fast Foods

Obtain a brochure from your favorite fast food restaurant which lists the nutrients contained in the various foods they serve. (The information is also available on the restaurant's own web site, or a web site such as the USDA or http://www.fatcalories.com/. Many health care providers also have a booklet listing the most popular foods.)

Pick out your favorite meal from your favorite fast food restaurant. List the foods on the chart. Then look up the calories, carbohydrates, protein, sodium and fat content of each item. Compare this to daily recommendations for each of the categories. What percentage are you getting in just one meal? Is this a good choice? (See "Facts to Remember" handout.)

Favorite Menu Items	Calories	Protein	Carbohydrate	Sodium	Fat
Totals					
Percent of Daily Requirements					

Your thoughts:

_____

Now select a healthier choice. Fill in all the categories and see how they compare. (You can use the same restaurant or select another restaurant.)

Favorite Menu Items	Calories	Protein	Carbohydrate	Sodium	Fat
Totals					
Percent of Daily Requirements					

Your thoughts:

Mommy, I'm Hungry! **Chapter 4**

Facts to Remember

Teens 14-18 years old should be eating

- about 2200 calories each day
- 46 grams of protein
- 130 grams of carbohydrates
- 66 grams of fat

Pregnant teens need

- 2600 calories each day
- 50-70 grams of protein
- 175 grams of carbohydrates
- 66 grams of fat

Breastfeeding mothers should have

- about 3000 calories per day
- 60-70 grams of protein
- 210 grams of carbohydrates
- 78 grams of fat

Children under six months

need all of their calories to come from breastmilk or formula.

Children from six to 12 months

still need their breastmilk or formula as their main source of nutrition.
Toward the end of her first year, your baby may be eating
2 1/2 containers of baby food or 1 1/4 cups of home-prepared food each day.

Toddlers from one to three years old need

- 1500 calories each day
- 13 grams of protein
- 130 grams of carbohydrates
- 35 grams of fat

Children from four to eight need

- 1700 calories each day
- 19 grams of protein
- 130 grams of carbohydrates
- 47 grams of fat

Mommy, I'm Hungry! Chapter 4
Fast Food Project

Obtain a nutrition chart from your favorite fast food restaurant. Now plan three fast food meals for you and two for your child that are fairly good for you and your child. Include the amount of fat, protein, carbohydrates (carbs), salt (sodium), and calories in each meal. Follow the way the meals were analyzed in this chapter. Note: Protein, carbohydrate, and fat are measured in grams, while sodium (salt) is listed in milligrams. Do not use the same menus as those in the book.

Menu #1	Calories	Protein	Carbs	Fat	Sodium
Totals Restaurant:					

Menu #2	Calories	Protein	Carbs	Fat	Sodium
Totals Restaurant:					

Menu #3	Calories	Protein	Carbs	Fat	Sodium
Totals Restaurant:					

Menu #1 - Child	Calories	Protein	Carbs	Fat	Sodium
Totals Restaurant:					

Menu #2 - Child	Calories	Protein	Carbs	Fat	Sodium
Totals Restaurant:					

Mommy, I'm Hungry! **Chapter 4**
Puzzle © by Edie De Avila

4. Fast Foods and Healthy Eating

Circle the <u>underlined</u> <u>words</u> in our grid. You can find them by
looking up, down, forward, backward, and diagonally.

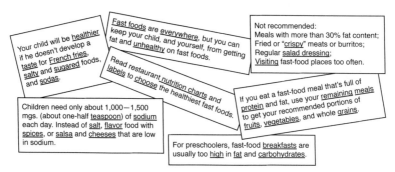

<u>Fast foods</u> are <u>everywhere</u>, but you can keep your child, and yourself, from getting <u>fat</u> and <u>unhealthy</u> on fast foods.

Your child will be <u>healthier</u> if he doesn't develop a <u>taste</u> for <u>French fries</u>, <u>salty</u> and <u>sugared</u> foods, and <u>sodas</u>.

<u>Read</u> restaurant <u>nutrition</u> <u>charts</u> and <u>labels</u> to <u>choose</u> the <u>healthiest</u> fast foods.

Not recommended:
Meals with more than 30% fat content;
Fried or "<u>crispy</u>" meats or burritos;
Regular <u>salad</u> dressing;
<u>Visiting</u> fast-food places too often.

Children need only about 1,000—1,500 mgs. (about one-half <u>teaspoon</u>) of <u>sodium</u> each day. Instead of <u>salt</u>, <u>flavor</u> food with <u>spices</u>, or <u>salsa</u> and <u>cheeses</u> that are low in sodium.

If you eat a fast-food meal that's full of <u>protein</u> and fat, use your <u>remaining</u> <u>meals</u> to get your recommended portions of <u>fruits</u>, <u>vegetables</u>, and whole <u>grains</u>.

For preschoolers, fast-food <u>breakfasts</u> are usually too <u>high</u> in <u>fat</u> and <u>carbohydrates</u>.

```
S T R A H C N O I T I R T U N A E S O O H C
A B L C E S B R E A K F A S T S T S V C R H
L C R A N I E T O R P S C S A L O F E H E E
A R E R E H W Y R E V E A R V D I D G E I T
D I M B F A S T F O O D S N I A T A A E H E
D S A O V Y H T L A E H N U P S E R F S T A
R R I H I D O S G R A I M O R P P Y R E L S
E O N Y S R L                 I S Y U S A P
S V I D I E S                 C G V I L E O
S A N R B S U                 E N I T R H O
I L G A A R G                 S I Y S C F N
N F L T I T A                 F T E R G R A
G R L E A R R                 R I V R R U A
S A F S B F E                 E S A O E S E
S P T C R I D                 H I G H L P H
V E G E T A B L E S A L A E T N V E A D I C
S U G A F R E N C H F R I E S I P S L A E M
```

Mommy, I'm Hungry! Chapter 4
Mini Case Studies

Caimile, p. 79, Text
Discussion Questions
1. How do you feel about the fast food advertising on television? Do you think it has an effect on what children eat?

2. Considering the time it takes to get ready to go, drive there, then wait for your order to be filled, is it always easier and quicker to go to McDonalds® than to cook at home?

3. Describe a meal you could fix at home in 15 minutes, a meal that would be more nutritious for your child than a hamburger, french fries, and soda.

Paige, pp. 90-91, Text
Discussion Questions
1. Paige describes herself as a fast food junkie. Why does she say this? Do you agree with her?

2. Consider Paige's idea of using the transaction approach to replacing fast food meals. What does she mean? Give an example of this approach.

3. What does having a child have to do with Paige's changed attitude toward fast food?

Nutrient Jigsaw Puzzle Directions

(Idea from Diane Smallwood)

There will be a total of fifteen different nutrient puzzles spaced out over the next six chapters. Keep an envelope at school big enough to hold the puzzle pieces without folding. Your teacher will tell you where to put the envelope at the end of class.

First, carefully cut the puzzle pieces apart as shown by the lines. Then put the pieces back together as you would a jigsaw puzzle. As you do so, concentrate on learning about the nutrient — the reason you need it in your diet and the best sources for the nutrient.

At the close of each jigsaw puzzle-making day, put all jigsaw puzzle pieces in your individual envelope and put away as requested by your teacher. You will receive your last jigsaw puzzle pieces as you study chapter 10.

On the day a new jigsaw puzzle is distributed, pick up your puzzle envelope, dump out the pieces, and fit all those already collected together as well as the new pieces. This is a good way to review the nutrient information.

You will have an extra quiz over this information after studying chapter 10, *Mommy, I'm Hungry!*

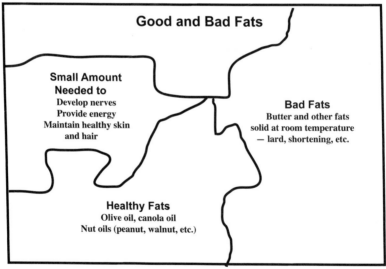

Good and Bad Fats

Small Amount Needed to
Develop nerves
Provide energy
Maintain healthy skin
and hair

Bad Fats
Butter and other fats
solid at room temperature
— lard, shortening, etc.

Healthy Fats
Olive oil, canola oil
Nut oils (peanut, walnut, etc.)

Mommy, I'm Hungry! Comprehensive Curriculum Notebook   81

Mommy, I'm Hungry! Chapter 4

Let's Cook Tonight

Characters: Seth, 17, and Sophie, 16, parents of Lea, 2

Sophie	That meal was great, Seth. Thanks! I love going to McDonalds®. But Seth, I'm getting fat! My pants barely button. *(She's almost in tears.)*
Seth	Well . . . I love you like you are. But I should tell you — I can't believe it, but my clothes are getting tight too. What's wrong with us? My grandma thinks I don't eat *enough*. You know how she's always giving us cookies and stuff. It's all her fault!
Sophie	I like your grandma and I love her cookies. So does Lea, and I worry about her getting chubby. But I don't think it's all your grandma's fault. Besides, I bet we could tell your grandma how much we love her, even without cookies. Well, not without cookies entirely, but maybe not so often or as many. She might *want* to help us.
Seth	I suppose we could do that. If we explain, I don't think it will hurt her feelings.
Sophie	But what about all those fast foods we've been eating? Remember that movie we saw? "Super Size Me" I think it was. Remember what happened to that man?
Seth	Yes, but he ate fast food all the time, for every meal. We don't do that.
Sophie	Yes, but we've stopped at McDonalds® fairly often lately. Those fries are so-o-o good.
Seth	I suppose we could give up the fries. McDonalds® does have other foods now. But that will be hard. I walk in that place, and suddenly I'm starving for a hamburger and fries, plus a soda, of course.
Sophie	My teacher told us about a way to fix french fries without cooking them in grease. I have an idea — how about if we fix our own dinner tonight? My mom is going out for dinner, and she won't mind if we cook. Let's make those "fries."
Seth	I don't know. Fries without the grease doesn't sound right. No flavor. But I suppose we could try it. As long as we have hamburgers, too. Don't forget the hamburgers.
Sophie	And what about all those sodas we drink? Do you know a 12-ounce can of soda contains *9 teaspoons* of sugar? That's another reason we're gettting fat. How about skim milk tonight?
Seth	Okay by me.
Sophie	I have an idea there, too. Let's go shopping. Have you tried hamburgers made of ground turkey? Suzie said that's what her mom uses because there's so much less fat in turkey than in hamburger. It tastes great. I'll even make us a salad if you'll cook the burgers.
Seth	Sounds like a plan. And here I was going to invite you to dinner at McDonalds again. But I'm willing to try this at least once.
Sophie	This will be a great meal for Lea, too. I'd even like to try slicing fresh fruit into plain yogurt for dessert. She loves it, and I think we'll like it, too.

See recipes for home-cooked "fast" food, p. 83 —
Burgers, non-greasy french fries, garlic salad.

Recipes — Let's Cook Tonight

Cajun "Fries" — 4 servings

2 baking potatoes	2 egg whites	1 T. Cajun spice

- Preheat oven to 400°.
- Peel and cut the potatoes into 1/4 inch slices. Then cut each slice into thin sticks and dry with paper towels.
- Combine lightly beaten egg whites with 1 T. Cajun spice in a bowl. Put the potato sticks in the bowl and mix until coated.
- Spray vegetable oil on a baking sheet.
- Arrange the potatoes in a single layer on the baking sheet. Leave a little space between pieces.
- Put the baking sheet on the bottom rack of the oven and bake 40-45 minutes. While they bake, turn them with a spatula every 6-8 minutes. You want them to brown evenly.

  They taste good, with a fraction of the calories in the greasy fast food fries.
  And don't forget the ketchup.

Turkey Burgers — 4 servings

Ground turkey contains less fat than hamburger — much healthier.

1 pound ground turkey	1 pkg. dry onion soup	1/4 cup water

Chopped onions, pepper, celery, etc., if desired

- Lightly mix the soup mix and water into the ground turkey. Add the chopped vegetables.
- Shape into four burgers.
- Grill outside, or on an indoor grill, or fry in a skillet very lightly sprayed with cooking oil.
- Place on a whole wheat bun. Add ketchup, mustard, sliced tomatoes, sliced onions, pickles.

  You could also cook sliced mushrooms in 1 t. of vegetable oil and place on hamburgers.

Jeanne's Salad — 4 servings

Dressing:

3 cloves garlic, minced	1/2 t. salt	1/2 t. pepper
3 T. Balsamic vinegar	1 T. olive oil	

- Mince or crush the garlic. Mash salt and pepper into the garlic.
- Add vinegar and mix well. Add oil. Stir or shake before using.
- Can be made in quantity and used for several meals.

Salad Mix:

6 mushrooms sliced	1 carrot thinly sliced
1/4 large red onion, thinly sliced	1 tomato cut into chunks
1/2 bunch dark green lettuce, torn into bite-size pieces	

- Combine the vegetables.
- Pour dressing over them and mix. (Best to add dressing right before eating.)

  Of course you can use whatever vegetables you like —
  small pieces of cauliflower, broccoli florets, sliced zucchini, green, red or yellow bell pepper,
  Chinese peas, frozen peas (thawed but not cooked), radishes, green onions, chopped jicama —
  the more variety the better!

Mommy, I'm Hungry! Quiz — Chapters 3 and 4

TRUE/FALSE. Write "T" before the sentence if it is true. Write "F" before it if it is false.

___ 1. Infants need small meals, but need to eat often.

___ 2. It's easy to find a healthy breakfast for a toddler at a fast food restaurant.

___ 3. It's okay to offer your baby several new foods each week.

___ 4. When you prepare food for your baby, you should not add salt or other seasonings.

___ 5. Baby's food should be warmed only to room temperature.

___ 6. Always insist that your baby eat everything you offer him.

___ 7. If you buy Stage 1 baby food, be sure to include the baby desserts.

___ 8. Feeding an infant honey can cause botulism (food poisoning).

___ 9. It is possible to order and eat healthy meals at some fast food restaurants.

___ 10. Babies need completely smooth food until they are a year old.

MULTIPLE CHOICE. Circle the letter of *all* the correct answers.

11. It is okay to put the following liquids in baby's bottle:
   a. Formula.
   b. Water.
   c. Orange juice.
   d. Cereal mixed with milk.

12. Eating too much salt can cause
   a. high blood pressure.
   b. toxemia in pregnancy.
   c. pneumonia.
   d. all of the above.

13. Fast foods that are *not* healthy include:
   a. fried or "crispy" meats.
   b. salads with low fat dressing.
   c. double burgers.
   d. fruit cup.

14. Foods labeled Low Carb
   a. are always good healthy choices.
   b. may be high in fat.
   c. may contain lots of calories.
   d. often contain too much sugar.

15. Fast food meals often provide too much
   a. carbohydrate.
   b. vitamin A.
   c. salt.
   d. fat.

SHORT ANSWERS

16-19. If you eat a chicken sandwich, salad, and a glass of milk at a fast food restaurant, what do you need to include in your other meals that day? Name four things.

1. _____

2. _____

3. _____

4. _____

20. Why is iron-enriched rice cereal a good choice for baby's first solid food?

21-22. You should give your baby no more than ____ cup of apple or pear juice.

How should you serve the juice?

23. Why should a baby never have coffee, tea, soda, or fruit drinks?

24. Why are french fries not good for a baby?

25-30. Write an essay in which you assume you have been eating a lot of fast foods. Explain why you should probably cut back on the fast foods. Then describe a plan for doing so. Be specific, and choose a plan that might really work for you.

Fast Foods and Healthy Eating

Student Objectives

1. Describe three fast food meals that are fairly nutritious.
2. Discuss strategies for cutting back on one's consumption of fast foods.
3. Explain the risks of eating too much salt.

Please read pp. 78-91 and answer the following questions.

1. Which "vegetable" is eaten more than any other vegetable by children aged 15 to 18 months? *French fries.*

   Why is this food not considered a real vegetable by some people? *Because they are so greasy and salty.*

2. What are you teaching your baby when you offer him a french fry? *I am teaching him to like the fat and salt in french fries.*

3. Is it possible to order and eat healthy meals at some fast food restaurants? *Yes.*

4. Complete the following chart showing nutrient needs:

	Calories	Protein	Carbs	Fat
Teens	2200	46	130	66
Pregnant teens	2600	50-70	175	66
Breastfeeding teen	3000	60-70	210	78
Toddler 1-3 years	1500	13	130	35
Child 4-8 years	1700	19	130	47

5. Why is it important not to eat a lot of salt (sodium)? *Eating too much salt contributes to high blood pressure and, in pregnancy, to toxemia (eclampsia).*

6. How much sodium does one teaspoon of salt contain? *2300 milligrams.*

   How much sodium should an adult consume in a day? *1500-2400 milligrams.*

7. What can you use in place of salt to make foods taste good? *Use spices, salsa, pepper, and other seasonings. Use low-sodium cheese such as Swiss cheese.*

8. Analyze the meals for Mom described on pp. 85-87 of your text. Which of these menus appeals to you? *Personal response.*

9. Even if you choose these fairly healthy fast food meals, what do you need to include in your eating for the rest of the day? *Drink more milk, eat at least four or five servings of fruits and vegetables, and several one-ounce servings of whole grains.*

10. Do you think most toddlers would enjoy the meal at the bottom of p. 87? Why or why not? *Personal response.*

Mommy, I'm Hungry! Comprehensive Curriculum Notebook

11. Why is it *not* a good idea to buy a toddler's breakfast at a fast food place? *It will be too high in fat and carbohydrates.*

12. List five fast foods absolutely *not* recommended.
    1. Any meal with more than 30 percent fat content.
    2. All fried or "crispy" meats or burritos.
    3. "Double" or "triple" sandwiches.
    4. Salads with crispy meats or regular salad dressings.
    5. Breakfast choices that include meat or eggs because they contain about 50 percent fat.

13. Are foods labeled "Low Carb" or "Low Fat" likely to be healthy choices? Why or why not?
    Probably not because Low Carb foods are often very high in fat and calories, while Low Fat items contain more carbs and may also be high in calories.

14. Describe three of the ways Paige managed to cut way back on her fast food eating.
    1. She would replace a fast food meal with something good. 2. She would take roads she knew would not take her past a fast food restaurant. 3. She figured out how much the fast food was costing her and realized she would rather spend that money some other way.

15. Pick three of the tips on p. 91 for cutting back on fast foods, three that you might try to follow. *Personal response, but answer may include three of the following:*
    1. Plan what you will order before you go.
    2. Pick up the food before you pick up the kids.
    3. Order, pick up at the drive-through window.
    4. Get away from the restaurant to eat the food.
    5. Avoid super-size items.
    6. Occasionally share a treat as a family, such as a small order of French fries which you share.

Writing Assignment

Count the number of fast food restaurants within two miles of your home and/or your school. Then write an essay in which you discuss the effect these fast food restaurants have on the teens who live in your area.

Project

Obtain a nutrition chart from your favorite fast food restaurant. Now plan three fast food meals for you and two for your child that are fairly good for you and your child. Include the amount of fat, protein, carbohydrates, salt, and calories in each meal. Follow the way the meals were analyzed in this chapter. Do not use the same menus as those in the book.
Note to teacher: See chart in Workbook.

Please take the quiz for chapters 3 and 4.

Mommy, I'm Hungry! **Chapter 4**

Quiz — Chapters 3-4. 1-T; 2-F; 3-F; 4-T; 5-T; 6-F; 7-F; 8-T; 9-T; 10-F; 11-a, b; 12-a, b; 13-a, c; 14-b, c; 15-a, c, d; 16-19- whole grains, fruits, vegetables, dairy products; 20-not likely to cause allergies; 21-22-1/4 cup, mix with same amount of water; 23-contain caffeine and/or sugar; 24-too greasy and salty; 25-30-essay covering plan for cutting back on eating of fast foods.

**Fast Foods
and Healthy Eating
Puzzle
Answer Key**

Discussion questions for "Let's Cook Tonight," p. 82.

1. Discuss the reasons Seth and Sophie are gaining weight.

2. How may their eating habits affect their daughter's health?

3. Suggest another practical, reasonable way they could improve their diets.

Playing with him encourages him to want to please you.

6

Teaching (Disciplining) with R.E.S.P.E.C.T

Reality
Environment
Self-esteem
Patience
Energy
Creativity
Trust

Ask your students to brainstorm the connection between each word in the acrostic and good discipline for babies and toddlers. They'll probably come up with some of the following concepts — and more:

Reality — Explain the importance of understanding the child's Reality (developmental stage).

Environment — Child-proofing the baby's Environment is a big factor in good discipline.

Self-esteem — Positive discipline will not tear down a child's

Self-esteem. Parents with good Self-esteem usually discipline more effectively.

Patience — Caring for a toddler takes huge amounts of Patience.

Energy refers both to the high Energy level of the child and the tremendous amount of Energy the parent needs to discipline effectively without losing his/her cool.

Creativity — A big dose of Creativity is important in designing discipline strategies.

Trust — For discipline to go well, parent and child must Trust each other.

Put them all together and they spell **RESPECT.**

Respect — The Foundation of Good Discipline

Respect for the child is the foundation of good discipline.

When a child is treated with respect, discipline (teaching) is not likely to be a big problem. Yet adults often show a lack of respect for little people.

If we just remember to treat them as "small people," like being polite to them. Yelling at them all the time can be just as wrong as abusing them physically.

Thelma, 20 - Melissa, 4; Janeen, 18 months

For a teen, grappling with the trauma of adolescence, maintaining respect for this little being who has changed the parent's life so drastically is often difficult.

Most discipline books are written for the parents of preschoolers or older children and ignore babies and toddlers. If your students' children are under three, methods for disciplining older children aren't very important yet. They need help in guiding their baby's behavior *now*.

The discipline methods parents use during the first three years have a big influence on the child's future behavior. This is a period of rapid change and learning. As parents guide that learning in a positive way, they are truly disciplining their child. That is what this chapter and the book, *Discipline from Birth to Three*, is about.

I have worked with hundreds of teenage parents who all wanted the best for their children. As we talked in the parenting classes and in the infant center, the question of discipline came up many times. Too often, "discipline" seemed to mean punishment. The young parents themselves had been punished for misdeeds for as long as they could remember. They knew no other way to handle their child. Most had never had a chance to learn self-control. Their parents had tried to control their lives by punishing them.

Discipline means to educate. If you're teaching teen parents, you have a wonderful opportunity to help them learn to educate their children, to help their children learn to behave, without punishment. It begins with trust. By meeting their child's needs in a loving, caring way, they will teach her to trust both her parents and her environment.

If your student helps her toddler satisfy his curiosity and comforts him when he is frustrated, he will learn that he is loved and respected. He doesn't have to be naughty to get attention. This kind of education is the foundation for the self-discipline the child will need throughout his life.

Discipline from Birth to Three (Lindsay and McCullough) is written to teenage parents, people who must blend their own needs as adolescents with the tremendous needs of their children.

The first three years of a person's life are judged by many experts to be the most important years in one's development. It is during these years that parents can teach their children a sense of self-worth and a positive approach to the world that will lessen discipline and life problems in later years. Yet it is in this crucial period in their children's lives that teenage parents must cope with their own developmental needs as adolescents. Combining their own needs with those of their children is indeed a huge challenge.

Discipline Is Teaching

The underlying concept of *Discipline from Birth to Three* is that discipline is teaching, not punishment. Punishment should have little if anything to do with teaching a child below age 3. If this concept is followed with the young child, punishment may never need to be a big part of that child's development. Young parents express their feelings on this issue.

Wendy isn't old enough to understand anything I tell her. If I tell her "No," she doesn't know what I mean. If she's doing something I don't want, I take it away from her and give her something else.

Pati, 21 - Wendy, 10 months

Young parents involved in their own developmental needs may find these concepts hard to understand.

Sometimes a young mother suggests that her baby cries "because he wants to upset me." The authors of *Discipline from Birth to Three* stress that babies cry because they need something. Responding to her baby's cries is the best approach, and will not result in a "spoiled" infant.

Start with Students' Realities

When I was in college, I was under the illusion that when we studied child development, we were mostly interested in middle-class, two-parent families where Mom stays home with the baby while Dad goes to work every day.

This is not the reality for the majority of families today. More than half the children in the United States now spend at least part of their childhood in a one-parent family. At least one-fourth of the children in the United States live below the poverty level. The percentage is higher among families started by a teenage parent.

If we are to help our students, we must understand their realities — without stereotyping "all teen parents are . . ." Teen parents come from all ethnic groups and socioeconomic levels. Most need special help. Each needs to be respected and treated as the unique individual s/he is.

The realities of teen parents' lives often is not "like it's supposed to be." For example, we know:

- *Build trust by responding* — but Grandma says, "You'll spoil that baby."

- *A peaceful home is needed* — but the home may hold lots of people, with room for little peace.

- *Don't rush solid food* — but Grandma, or perhaps a neighbor, says, "That child is hungry. He needs real food!" at 3 months.

- *Reading to children is important* — but there may be no books, magazines, or newspapers in the home, and no one else reads.

- *Calm bedtime is essential* — but perhaps other small children sleep in the same room with the baby and their bedtime is later.

- *Curiosity is crucial, so childproof your home* — but the teen parent's mom and dad are convinced that babies "need to be taught" not to touch things.

- *Limit television viewing* — but the TV is constantly on.

- *Outlaw junk food* — but parents and other family members may not model good eating habits.

- *Don't hit children* — but those around the parent insist the toddler will be spoiled if he's not spanked.

- *Don't rush toilet teaching* — but Grandma says, "When you were 10 months old, you were trained."

Changing habits is hard for most of us. For a teen to attempt to change the habits of those around him may be practically impossible. Instead, we need to focus on helping him figure out how to deal with what is, and parent well in spite of these situations.

You might start by discussing the above comments with young parents. How do/would they deal with these issues?

Disciplining Infants

A big part of dealing with reality is the fact that disciplining an infant means the parents must be disciplined, not the baby. The baby's job during those first months is to learn to trust those around him, and to learn the world is a good place to be. His parents' job is to meet his needs as completely as possible — even as they do their best to meet their own needs, too.

If the baby cries, it is not because he is trying to be difficult. It's because he needs something — even if he has just been fed, had his diaper changed, and is warm. Tell your students to imagine:

You are an infant and you can't move out of your crib. You're dry, warm, and you've been fed, but you're lonely. You cry but nobody responds. How do you feel?

Ask students to perform dramatically the skit from chapter 1, pp. 29-30, "Babies Don't Spoil," then discuss. In the skit, actors are infants who are trying to figure out what "spoil" means and why this seems to be a problem with some parents.

Environment Takes Planning

When the baby becomes a crawler, then a toddler, the environment becomes especially important. Childproofing the home can prevent a lot of discipline problems. Removing items baby should not touch and things that could harm him is vital.

Electric outlets need to be covered, and valuable books and other items placed out of reach of the toddler. But emptying the rooms of everything except the furniture is not necessary either. Bookshelves for the child's books and toys will help her handle, mouth, and play with things as she should, without destroying other people's things. She needs plenty of opportunities to satisfy her budding curiosity.

If your client lives with his or her parents, childproofing may be difficult. If grandparents say the child needs to learn not to touch things, what can the young parent do?

Focusing on the safety of the child is a good approach. Grandparents who "don't believe" in childproofing don't want the child hurt. Putting an antique glass vase on the coffee table, then expecting the child not to touch it, is crazy. They don't want the vase broken, and if it is dropped, glass shards on the floor can hurt the child.

If the teen parent has a room of her own, perhaps that can be childproofed, and parent and child can spend a lot of time there. Sometimes the grandparent agrees to let the parent put up things the child shouldn't touch while they are in the room, but leave items out the rest of the time.

If there is a safe place for the child and parent to play outdoors, he can spend some of his energy and satisfy some of his curiosity there.

Also discuss the importance of creating a stimulating environment for the child. He doesn't need boxes and boxes of toys, but he does need playthings that will help him learn about his world.

Self-Esteem and Discipline

Discipline will go better if both parent and child have healthy self-esteem. The parent who hears from everyone around her that she is a poor parent probably is — but mostly because that's what she has been taught. It's known as a self-fulfilling prophecy. To parent well, she has to be convinced that she can.

Your job is to help her learn how to parent effectively, and to be sure she knows when she is doing well with her child. Having good self-esteem frees her to discipline more effectively.

The child whose needs are met most of the time from birth, and whose parents and others frequently express how much they love and admire him is likely to feel pretty good about himself. This is likely to translate into a child who wants to please Mom and Dad, an important part of the discipline arena.

Patience Required

Adolescents and patience are not an easy mix, yet parents of babies and toddlers must have an unending supply of patience as they deal with their little ones. Being part of a group can help. As two parents talk with each other about their frustrations, and they find they are not alone, they may be able to build some of that necessary patience.

If they aren't allowed to childproof at home, for example, how do they handle the toddler's constant reaching for forbidden things? Help them realize that shouting at him from across the room simply won't work.

Each time he heads for that forbidden object, the parent needs to get up and move him away, perhaps substitute a toy. But the patience needed for utilizing this necessary technique probably seems unreal to some parents. Yet in the long run, handling such situations with patience will result in a far better relationship between parent and child.

Young parents also need to realize how little patience a child has. If Mom's on the phone, he wants her attention *now*. If he is ready to go outside and Dad isn't, he has a fit. And so it goes. The parent is the one who must develop patience in the early months and years.

Energy for Parent and Child

A very young parent may have more energy than an older parent, a definite advantage in the intense job of parenting. Trying to keep up with a two-year-old is a wild assignment. When we are older, sometimes we wonder if all that energy is wasted on someone who's only two!

Not only is it hard simply to keep up with a toddler. Add effective discipline/teaching into the mix, and the parent has quite a challenge.

Help your clients understand how important their own health is. Eating appropriate amounts of nutritious food and getting enough rest helps a parent cope with the huge task of parenting.

Getting enough rest may be a fantasy for adolescents who are parenting a child, going to school, and perhaps working part-time. Learning to plan ahead and make lists of tasks to be accomplished can help — as long as that list doesn't act as a discouraging "I can't do it" reminder.

Prioritizing is especially important — with the child having high priority in the parent's plan.

Creative Approach to Discipline

Good teachers are usually creative teachers. Good parents are creative in their approach to teaching toddlers. Saying "No" constantly doesn't work well. Neither does spanking. Far more effective is a positive approach. For a few months, the child can be diverted from unwanted behavior by substituting a toy or an activity.

Keeping him busy can help. If he watches much TV, he either watches it like a zombie, or his energy gets him into trouble. Limiting TV and guiding him to active play can work when a creative parent is involved in the process.

Telling the child stories and listening to his stories is important.

If the parent finger-paints with him, it's more fun. Making a game out of picking up toys makes it easier for him to help.

Ask your students to define creativity as it applies to parenting. Brainstorm examples.

Discuss the strategies listed below. Ask students to tie creative approaches into each of these strategies. You may be amazed at the great suggestions they make.

Ten Discipline Strategies that Work

1. **Distract Your Child** — Move her near toys she can have.

2. **Communication and Respect** — Discipline will be easier.

3. **Use "No" Sparingly** — Use only when it's likely to be effective.

4. **Use a Positive Approach** — Say "You need to . . ." and "You may not . . ."

5. **Consistent and Balanced Lifestyle** — Balance active and quiet play. Stick with eating and sleeping routine for child.

6. **Give Your Child a Choice** — Be sure you can live with the choices you give.

7. **Reinforce Behaviors You Like** — Praise works so much better than punishment.

8. **Warn Your Child Before Activity Changes** — She has time to adjust.

9. **Time Out May Help** — The goal is not to punish, but to get back in control.

10. **Provide a Reward** — Tell him he did a good job and that you are proud of him.

Trust Between Parent and Child

Trust between parent and child goes both ways. The infant's big job is to learn to trust her parents and others around her. She learns to trust through having her needs met and experiencing an unending supply of love. It's the parent who must be disciplined. Knowing that someone responds lovingly to baby's cries is a big part of learning to trust.

Building that trust, however, means the parent must trust the baby with some decisions. For example, baby knows when and how much he needs to eat. Does he seem hungry every hour or two those first weeks? Then he needs to be fed. If he's bottle fed, does he turn his head away from the bottle or show other signs of having enough? Then the parent should trust the baby's wisdom, and quit feeding him even though this means "wasting" the last ounce or two of formula. Baby knows how much food he needs.

Being consistent with a child plays a huge part in building trust and avoiding discipline problems. He basically wants to please his parents, but if one day they laugh at him for eating the sugar out of the sugar bowl, and the next day treat the same action as very bad, he's confused. Simple rules must be enforced. Just as important, those rules must be limited to the safety of the child and to other issues the parent considers truly important.

Trust goes the other way, too. The parent needs to trust the child to make decisions when possible. That is, they provide choices. Choices a toddler could make might be deciding which color shirt to wear, whether to have a shower or a bath, which book to read, etc. All choices offered must be choices the parent can accept.

To build trust, the parent needs to follow up on all promises to the child. Promises must not be made that the parent can't keep.

If the child lives with one parent, and the other visits occasionally, those visits need to happen as promised. Being told that Daddy will visit next Saturday, and then Daddy doesn't show up on Saturday can be devastating to a child's trust.

Classroom Teaching Plan

Curriculum for chapter 6, "Yelling, Spanking Don't Help," *Discipline from Birth to Three Comprehensive Curriculum Notebook*, is reproduced on pp. 172-178.

If you're teaching a daily class, and you're designing a week of classes focusing on this topic, you can utilize these assignments. For example:

Monday. Begin with a discussion of discipline. What does the word mean to your students? What are their goals in disciplining their children?

Then spend the rest of the period reading the chapter, either individually, or as a class. You and the students could take turns reading the chapter aloud, allowing time for commenting on concepts presented. Students might like to take turns reading the teen quotes while you read the other parts of the chapter. As you read, some of the quotes can be treated as mini case studies. What would your students do in similar siuations?

Finish the session by asking them to write in their journals, "My favorite time with my child is . . . because . . ." (activity #6).

Tuesday. Give each student a copy of "Yelling and Spanking Don't Help" (activity #2, p. 175). Discuss, and remind them to put this summary of the chapter in their notebooks.

Lead a class discussion on "Setting Limits with Respect" (activity #8). Ask them to discuss specific examples. You will need to have some examples ready to get them started. If there is time, assign an essay on this topic (activity #9).

For homework, ask each student to ask at least five parents of children under three how they feel about spanking (enrichment activity #1).

Wednesday. Give each student a copy of "Discipline Situations," p. 177 (activity #3). Discuss. You might ask students to role-play the situations described. Suggest they choose a discipline strategy from the "Child Guidance Techniques" chart (activity #1, p. 176), suitable for each situation as it is role-played.

Thursday. Field trip to an infant/toddler center where your students will observe gentle discipline techniques with babies and toddlers (enrichment activity #2).

OR

Organize a debate — "Resolved: Spanking Children Teaches Them to Behave Better" (activity #4). After the debate, discuss how the parents' feelings influence the way they discipline their children. Then ask students to complete the workbook assignment in which they write a paragraph explaining how their feelings are involved in the way they discipline. Ask them to describe a discipline problem that might not have happened if they were feeling better.

Friday. Have supplies ready to make the Pull-a-Cloth toy (activity #11, p. 178). Explain that this toy helps baby learn how to grasp items, and that they need to show the baby how to play with the toy.

Naturally you will adjust activities to fit your students and the length of each class session.

Not-for-Credit Group Sessions

If you spend only one session on this topic, you might start by discussing the handout, "Yelling and Spanking Don't Help" (activity #2, p. 175). Go on to "Discipline Situations" (activity #3, p. 177) with participants role-playing the various vignettes. Give each participant a copy of "Child Guidance Techniques" (activity #1, p. 176) and ask them to choose a strategy suitable for each situation role-played.

The next activity could be a discussion of the phrase, "Setting Limits with Respect" (activity #8) and/or ask the group to explain how their feelings influence how they discipline their children (activity #7).

You might conclude this session by talking about the role positive activities play in preventing discipline problems, then have supplies available for them to make the toy described in activity #11, p. 178. Ask them to show their child how to play with the Pull-a-Cloth toy.

Taking your group to a childcare center to observe gentle discipline strategies for babies and toddlers would also be a valuable learning experience.

Have books available for participants who wish to read more about this topic.

Home Visit Teaching

As a home visitor, you have an opportunity truly to listen to your client's ideas on discipline. If s/he is convinced that spanking is a necessary part of disciplining babies and toddlers, you need to discuss better methods of discipline even as you maintain respect for her thinking on the subject.

Many of us worry that spanking not only teaches children that big people can hit smaller ones, but also that spanking can too easily turn into child abuse. However, you will focus more on better methods of discipline, methods that are more likely to produce the results the parent wants.

Most valuable would be for your client to relate discipline problems she has observed with other parents and their children, or problems she has experienced with her child. Then you'd discuss with her possible strategies for dealing with these problems. You might also give her a copy of "Discipline Situations," p. 177, and ask how she might handle these happenings.

Discipline is a great challenge for almost all parents, and perhaps especially for very young parents. If you can help your clients/students move from punishing in anger to teaching with respect, you will make a great difference in the lives of both parent and child.

Teaching teen parents the art and skills of parenting, whether in the classroom, through independent study, in group sessions, or on home visits, is possibly the most relevant to clients' needs as well as the most challenging job you could have. *Enjoy!*

Topic: Spanking
Discipline from Birth to Three

Chapter 6

Yelling, Spanking Don't Help — pp. 86-99

Objective: Student will be able to

Explain in writing how little a child learns from being spanked or yelled at — except that spanking and yelling must be all right if you're big.

SUPPLEMENTARY RESOURCE

Field trip. Infant/toddler center to observe discipline techniques.

TEACHER PREPARATION — CHAPTER 6

1. **Review Chapter 6,** text, pp. 86-99, and the workbook assignments and suggested responses, p. 90 of this *Notebook.* Review the quiz over chapters 5 and 6, p. 89. Quiz key is on p. 90.

2. **Review the learning activities,** decide which ones you'll use, and reproduce the needed handouts for students. Suggested for this chapter are: "Yelling and Spanking Don't Help," p. 84; "Child Guidance Techniques" chart, p. 85; "Discipline Situations," p. 86; "Mini Case Studies from Text — Joanne, Raylene, Guadalupe" discussion questions, p. 87; "Toy for Your Child — Pull-a-Cloth," p. 88; Quiz over chapters 5 and 6, p. 89. **Write the Parent/Child Assignment on the board.**

3. **Schedule a field trip to an infant/toddler center.** Purpose is for your students to observe gentle discipline techniques with babies and toddlers.

4. **Be prepared to demonstrate making the Pull-a-Cloth toy,** p. 88. Ask students to collect materials for making this toy for their child — a three-pound coffee can and three lids plus large scraps of cloth with different textures (voil, velvet, tricot, satin, double knit, burlap, etc.). Or will a fabric store donate pieces of the various kinds of fabric? Take a sample of the toy with you along with your program brochure when you approach the store manager.

⚡CORE CURRICULUM — GROUP LEARNING

Reading Assignment (individually or together)
Chapter 6, *Discipline from Birth to Three,* "Yelling, Spanking Don't Help," pp. 86-99. **Discuss.** Workbook questions (pp. 13-14) can guide discussion. **Optional:** Students write individual or group responses to questions. See p. 90 for suggested responses to workbook assignments.

The P.A.R.E.N.T. Approach   173

LEARNING ACTIVITIES – CHAPTER 6

1. **Activity.** "Child Guidance Techniques" chart, page 85. Give each student a copy and ask them to respond to the questions.

2. **Handout.** Give each student a copy of "Yelling and Spanking Don't Help." Discuss; remind students to put handout in their notebooks.

3. **Class Discussion.** "Discipline Situations," p. 86. Give each student a copy, then discuss in class. You might ask students to role-play the situations described. Then suggest they choose a discipline strategy from the "Child Guidance Techniques" chart (#1 above) suitable for each situation as it is role-played.

4. **Debate.** Resolved: "Spanking children teaches them to behave better."

5. **Case Studies.** Joanne, pp. 89-90, Raylene, p. 93, Guadalupe, p. 99, text; discussion questions, page 87, *Notebook*. Or ask students to take turns reading the quotes in the chapter. Give them an opportunity to discuss each one.

6. **Journal.** Suggested starter: "My favorite time with my child is . . . because . . ."

7. **Writing Assignment** (Workbook). Write a paragraph in which you explain how your feelings influence how you discipline your child. Include examples of discipline problems that might not have happened if you had been feeling better.

8. **Class Discussion.** What does "setting limits with respect" mean to you? Ask students to discuss specific examples. Have some examples ready to get them started.

9. **Writing Assignment.** After the above discussion, write an essay on "Setting Limits with Respect."

10. **Quiz.** Chapters 5 and 6, p. 89.

11. **Toy Making.** Make a **Pull-a-Cloth toy,** p. 88. If students supply the coffee cans and lids, perhaps a local fabric store would donate the different kinds of cloth needed for this toy.

12. **Parent/Child Assignment.** Show your child how to play with the Pull-a-Cloth toy you made in class. Report on your experience in your journal.

ENRICHMENT ACTIVITIES

1. **Research** (Workbook). Ask each student to ask at least five parents of children under three how they feel about spanking. Were they spanked when they were little? What do they think spanking teaches a child? Compile results in class.

2. **Field Trip** (Workbook). Take your class to visit a childcare center. Tell students to observe the methods of discipline used by the caregivers. Do they see mostly positive discipline? Or is there a lot of scolding? How about other forms of punishment?

Discipline from Birth to Three Comprehensive Curriculum Notebook   82

*Reprinted with permission
from **Discipline from Birth to Three
Comprehensive Curriculum Notebook.**
Reduced to 60%. To reproduce at full size, enlarge to 150%.*

INDEPENDENT STUDY ASSIGNMENTS — CHAPTER 6

Topic: Spanking
Discipline from Birth to Three

Resources
Text: *Discipline from Birth to Three* and Workbook, Chapter 6

Handouts
"Yelling and Spanking Don't Help," p. 84.
"Child Guidance Techniques" chart, p. 85.
"Discipline Situations," p. 86.
"Mini Case Studies from Text — Joanne, Raylene, Guadalupe" discussion
   questions, p. 87.
"Toy for Your Child — Pull-a-Cloth," p. 88.
Quiz over chapters 5 and 6, p. 89.

1. **Read Chapter 6**, *Discipline from Birth to Three*, "Yelling, Spanking Don't Help," pp. 86-99. Complete assignments in Workbook (pp. 13-14) including the writing assignment and the projects.

2. **Write in your journal.** Suggested starter: "My favorite time with my child is . . . because . . ."

3. **Handout.** Read "Yelling and Spanking Don't Help," and place in your notebook.

4. **Activity.** Please respond to the questions on the "Child Guidance Techniques" chart.

5. **Discipline Situations.** Read "Discipline Situations," p. 86. In writing, explain what you would do in at least five of these situations. For each situation, choose an appropriate strategy from the "Child Guidance Techniques" chart.

6. **Case Studies.** Joanne, pp. 89-90, Raylene, p. 93, Guadalupe, p. 99, text. Respond to the attached discussion questions in writing.

7. **Writing Assignment.** What does "setting limits with respect" mean to you? In writing, discuss this concept along with specific examples.

8. **Quiz.** Please take the quiz over chapters 5 and 6.

9. **Toy Making.** Make a Pull-a-Cloth toy. See attached directions.

10. **Parent/Child Assignment.** Show your child how to play with the Pull-a-Cloth toy you made. Report on your experience in your journal.

Prepared by Deborah Cashen, author of *Creating Parenting Notebooks*

Discipline from Birth to Three — Chapter 6

Yelling and Spanking Don't Help

No one should ever discipline a child in anger.
If we want our children to respect other people, we have to show respect for them.
We must demonstrate the behavior we want them to imitate.

PARENTING ISN'T EASY

✓ In spite of all your good intentions, you may yell

at your child about what she is doing. Explain what

happened. Tell her you're sorry you yelled at her.

✓ How you feel about yourself influences how you discipline
your child.

✓ Be extra careful not to take your angry feelings out on your child.

✓ All parents get upset with their children, even their babies. If it gets to where
you are yelling and hitting your child because of your own frustrations, get help.

✓ Childrearing based on love and respect is more enjoyable for both parent and child.

✓ It is the job of parents to encourage, teach, and make exploring safe.

✓ Punishment interferes with learning. None of us learn when we are afraid.

✓ Blind obedience causes children to be followers who will do what other people tell
them to do without judging whether it's right or wrong.

SETTING LIMITS WITH RESPECT

✓ Stay thoughtful as a parent.

✓ Stay ahead of your child.

✓ Take time to figure out how your child feels and why he behaves the way he does.

✓ Taking time for this kind of thinking is a good start toward planning discipline
strategies that work without yelling, slapping, or hitting.

Love and Trust Your Child and Let Him Know You Do!

Discipline from Birth to Three, Chapter 6

Child Guidance Techniques

Developed by Bobbie Ackley

Problem behavior on the part of children can often be prevented if parents take the time to supervise children's activities and establish routines for daily experiences such as meals, naps, and bedtime. When problem behavior does occur, there are many ways to deal with the situation. Listed below are sixteen techniques many parents use when their children misbehave. Please check how often you use each technique with your child.

	Never	Seldom	Sometimes	Often	Always
1. Prevention					
2. Do nothing approach (Ignore misbehavior)					
3. Sympathize with child's frustration					
4. Remind					
5. Suggest					
6. Distract					
7. Tell child to stop (No-No)					
8. Scold (Tongue lashing)					
9. Threaten					
10. Carry out threat					
11. Take direct action to enforce orders					
12. Let child suffer the consequence (Let punishment fit the "crime")					
13. Isolate the child					
14. Loss of privileges (TV, grounded, etc.)					
15. Hit child with hand (F = on the face; H = on the hand; B = on the bottom)					
16. Beat child (Leave marks and/or use belt, stick, etc.)					

Suggestion for Teacher: After students have checked their choices above, share with them the situation descriptions on the following page. Which technique would they recommend for each?

Discipline from Birth to Three, Chapter 6 (Developed by Bobbie Ackley)

Discipline Situations

1. Tammy, 3, was quietly coloring on a big sheet of paper. You came into the room and scooped her up saying, "It's time for bed." Tammy begins kicking and screaming, shouting, "No!"

2. Dustin, 3, was busily playing in his sandbox. You go out to call him in for the evening and discover he has wet his pants.

3. Eric, 21/2, was stitting at the table eating his lunch. He picked up his glass of milk and moved it quickly toward his mouth. It spilled all over the table, floor, and Eric.

4. Jason, 3, was seated in the grocery cart while you were busy unloading the cart and placing items on the checkout counter. You turn to see Jason put a sucker from the counter display into his pocket.

5. You walk into the room and find Sophie, 2, playing with the buttons on your new television.

6. You overhear a racket in the living room and go to investigate. You find Michael, 21/2, sprawled on the floor kicking and crying because he is having difficulty with a puzzle.

7. Bobby, 21/2, and Jeannie, 2, are playing together in the den when you hear a scream. Bobby runs in crying, and shows you a welt where Jeannie bit him.

8. Kathi, 2, grabs a doll from her playmate, Steve. Steve starts to cry and tries to grab his doll back.

9. You carry Lee, 21/2, to bed and tuck him in for the night. When you start to leave the room and turn out the light, Lee begins crying. He says, "The monsters will get me."

10. You hear your new baby screaming, and you go in to investigate. You find Sam, 3, leaning over the cradle "hugging" the baby.

11. When you walked into the room, you found Kim, 2, drawing on the wall with magic markers she found on the counter.

12. Erin, 2, is hugging the kitten too tightly.

13. Pati, 21/2, has learned how to open the refrigerator door. She pulls things out and makes a mess.

14. You are ironing and Alex, 2, is determined to play at your feet. You are worried that she'll pull the iron down and get burned.

15. Kent, 2, eats half his cereal, then starts dumping the rest over the edge of his high chair.

16. Josh, 2, screams and refuses to cooperate when you try to buckle him into his carseat.

17. Lindsay and Nicole, two-year-old twins, constantly fight over their toys. They always want the same one at the same time.

18. Grandma has come to visit for the first time in a year. She is horrified to find that Travis, 2, will have nothing to do with her.

19. Lunch is ready, but Rachel, 3, says she doesn't want to eat. You know she'll be hungry soon and want junk food.

20. Mike, 2, constantly opens his dresser drawers and dumps his clothes out on the floor.

21. Will, 18 months, has a tantrum, apparently because you gave him a chicken leg instead of the wing he wanted.

22. Will has another tantrum because he wants candy before dinner, and you said "No."

Discipline from Birth to Three, Chapter 6

Toy for Your Child

Pull-a-Cloth

This toy may help baby learn to grasp items.

Materials
• One 3-pound coffee can
• Three lids to fit the can
• Eight to twelve large scraps of cloth (voile, velvet, tricot, satin, double knit, burlap, broadcloth, etc.)

Procedure
Be sure top edge of can is smooth. Going around the top of the can with a can opener a second time may smooth the edge.

In one coffee can lid, cut a round hole 2 1/2" in diameter. (The child's fist will be able to go through this hole.) In another lid, cut a hole 1 1/2" square. (This hole is large enough to encourage the child to grasp the cloth with his palm.)

In the other lid, cut an elliptical hole 3/4" by 2 1/2". (This shape will encourage thumb-finger pinching.)

Cut the cloth scraps 12" to 18" long and just narrow enough to pull through the hole. They should not come through the hole too easily.

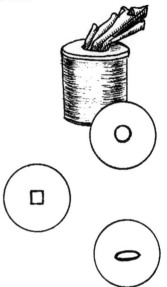

Appendix

About the Author

Jeanne Warren Lindsay is the author of twenty-one books for and about pregnant and parenting teens. More than 800,000 copies of her books had been sold by 2008. Her *Teen Dads: Rights, Responsibilities and Joys* was selected by the American Library Association as a Recommended Book for Reluctant Young Adult Readers.

Lindsay has worked with hundreds of pregnant and parenting teenagers. She developed the Teen Parent Program at Tracy High School, Cerritos, California, and coordinated the program for many years. Most of her books are written for pregnant and parenting teens, and quotes from interviewees are frequently used to illustrate concepts.

Lindsay grew up on a farm in Kansas. She has lived in the same house in Buena Park, California, for many years. She loves to visit the Middle West, but says she's now addicted to life in southern California. She has five grown children and seven grandchildren.

Lindsay is the editor of *PPT Express*, a quarterly newsletter for teachers and others working with pregnant and parenting teens. She speaks frequently at conferences across the country, and holds training sessions in her home for teen parent teachers. She says she's happiest while interviewing young people for her books or writing under the big avocado tree in her backyard.

Teens Parenting Curriculum

The *Teens Parenting* curriculum includes the following resources:

Your Pregnancy and Newborn Journey by Jeanne Warren Lindsay and Jean Brunelli. Also available in Easier Reading edition (grade level 2) and Spanish, *Tu embarazo y el nacimiento de tu bebé* + workbook and answer key for each edition. *Prenatal health book for pregnant teens. Includes section on care of newborn and chapter for fathers plus quotes from teens to reinforce concepts.*
Your Pregnancy and Newborn Journey Comprehensive Curriculum Notebook
Two-in-One Pregnancy Bingo, $24.95
Pregnancy and Newborn Journey Board Game, $34.95

Nurturing Your Newborn by Lindsay and Brunelli. Regular, GL 2, and Spanish (*Crianza del recién nacido)* + workbook (disposable or personalized on CD) and teacher's guide. Text: $7.95, 10/$50, 25/$100. *Focuses on postpartum period. Ideal for parents home after delivery.*

Your Baby's First Year: A Guide for Teenage Parents by Lindsay. Regular, GL2, and Spanish (*El primer año del bebé)* + workbook and answer key for each. *All about parenting during the first year with lots of input from teen parents.*
Nurturing Your Newborn/Baby's First Year Curriculum Notebook
Baby's First Year Board Game, $34.95
4-DVD series - Nurturing Your Newborn, She's Much More Active, Leaving Baby Stage Behind, Keeping Your Baby Healthy. $195

Mommy, I'm Hungry! Good Eating for Little Ones by Lindsay, Brunelli, and Sally McCullough. Regular and Spanish (*¡Mami, tengo hambre!)* + workbook and answer key for each. *Help for teen parents and their children on the crucial topic of nutrition. Includes chapters on fast foods and fat-proofing one's child.*
Mommy, I'm Hungry! Comprehensive Curriculum Notebook

Discipline from Birth to Three: How Teen Parents Can Prevent and Deal with Discipline Problems with Babies and Toddlers by Lindsay and McCullough. Regular, GL2, and Spanish *(La disciplina hasta los tres años)* + workbook and answer key for each. *Provides teenage parents with guidelines to help prevent discipline problems with children, and for dealing with problems when they occur.*
Discipline from Birth to Three Comprehensive Curriculum Notebook
Discipline from Birth to Three Board Game, $34.95
4-DVD series, Discipline from Birth to Three, $195

The Challenge of Toddlers: For Teen Parents — Parenting Your Child from One to Three by Lindsay. Regular and Spanish *(El reto de los párvulos)* + workbooks and answer keys. *All about parenting during the toddler years.*
The Challenge of Toddlers Comprehensive Curriculum Guide
Challenge of Toddlers Board Game, $34.95

Teen Dads: Rights, Responsibilities and Joys + workbook and teacher's guide. *A how-to-parent book especially for teenage fathers. Offers help in parenting from conception to age 3 of the child. Many quotes from and photos of teen fathers.*
Teen Dads Comprehensive Curriculum Notebook

Pricing: When purchased separately, each of the texts above (except *Nurturing Your Newborn)* is $12.95; 10/$120; 25/$275. Workbooks, $2.50, 10/$20, 25/$40. Quantity discount for first six texts combined, $67, 10 sets/$620, 25 sets/$1425. Six workbooks, $12.95, 10 sets/$110, 25 sets/$212.50. **Comprehensive Curriculum Notebooks,** $125 each, all six, $625. (**Note: See p. 20 for general *Notebook* contents.**)

For the teacher/leader:

The P.A.R.E.N.T. Approach: How to Teach Young Moms and Dads the Art and Skills of Parenting by Lindsay. $12.95.

ROAD to Fatherhood: How to Help Young Dads Become Loving and Responsible Parents by Jon Morris. $14.95. *Along with teen fathers' real stories, the book is a guide for teachers, counselors, social workers developing comprehensive services for young fathers.*

The Softer Side of Hip-Hop: Poetic Reflections on Love, Family and Relationships by Laura Haskins-Bookser. $9.95. Teacher's guide, $4.95. *A teen mom shares her pain, frustrations, and joys as she parents her child.*

Read to Me! I Will Listen: Tips Mom and Dad Can Use to Help Me Become a Lifelong Reader by Nancy Kelly Allen. $2.95, 10/$25, 25/$50; 100/$150. Free teacher's guide. *Perfect supplement for parenting course.*

Complete Teens Parenting Curriculum $1236.00
One copy of everything listed here
(choose one edition of titles available
in regular, Spanish and Easier Reading)

Bibliography

The following bibliography contains books, websites, and DVDs of interest to young parents. Prices are quoted for the resources, but because prices change so rapidly, call your local or Internet book store or your local library reference department for an updated price and address before ordering a book. See pages 191-192 for an order form for Morning Glory Press publications.

Day, Alexandra. *Good Dog, Carl.* 1997. 32 pp. $6.99. Aladdin.
Wonderful book about Carl, the rottweiler, who takes care of the baby. Check the other titles in this almost wordless series.

Haskins-Bookser, Laura. *Dreams to Reality — Help for Young Moms: Education, Career and Life Choices.* 2006. 176 pp. $14.95. Personal Journal, $3.00. Morning Glory Press.
Young mom's story along with many tips and information about following one's dreams, whether it be going to college, a career, travel, etc.

Johnson, Angela. *The First Part Last.* 2004. 144 pp. $5.99. Simon Pulse.
Story of teenage dad, with alternate chapters of "Then" and "Now." Good.

Lansky, Vicki. *Games Babies Play from Birth to Twelve Months.* 2001. 100 pp. $10.95. Book Peddlers.
Many ideas for helping parents interact with their children in creative ways.

Leach, Penelope. *Your Baby and Child from Birth to Age Five.*
Revised, 1997. 560 pp. $20. Alfred A. Knopf.
An absolutely beautiful book packed with information, many color photos
and lovely drawings. Comprehensive, authoritative, and outstandingly
sensitive guide to child care and development.

Lindsay, Jeanne Warren. *Do I Have a Daddy? A Story About a Single-*
Parent Child. 2000. 48 pp. Paper, $7.95. Free study guide. Morning
Glory Press.
A beautiful full-color picture book for the child who has never met his/her
father. A special sixteen-page section offers suggestions to single mothers.

_____. *Pregnant? Adoption Is an Option.* 1996. 224 pp. $11.95.
Teacher's Guide, Study Guide, $2.50 each. Morning Glory Press.
Birthparents share stories of responsible, difficult adoption planning. Does
*not "push" adoption, but suggests **planning** and deliberate decision-making.*
Stresses open adoption and birthparents' role in choosing adoptive parents.

Marecek, Mary. *Breaking Free from Partner Abuse.* 1999. 96 pp.
$8.95. Quantity discount. Morning Glory Press.
Lovely edition illustrated by Jami Moffett. Underlying message is that the
reader does not deserve to be hit. Simply written. Can help a young woman
escape an abusive relationship.

MELD Parenting Materials. *The New Middle of the Night Book:*
Answers to Young Parents' Questions When No One Is Around.
1999. 163 pp. $12.50. MELD, Suite 507, 123 North Third Street,
Minneapolis, MN 55401.
Includes clearly written information about parenting during the first two
years of life. An especially good section discusses the benefits and how-tos
of shared parenting, whether or not the parents are together as a couple.

Pantley, Elizabeth. *The No-Cry Sleep Solution: Gentle Ways to*
Help Your Baby Sleep Through the Night. 2002. 108 pp. $15.95.
Also *The No-Cry Sleep Solution for Toddlers and Preschoolers.*
McGraw-Hill.
Both books offer positive approaches to help babies and toddlers get to bed,
stay in bed, and sleep through the night.

Parent Express: A Month-By-Month Newsletter for You and Your
Baby. 15 8-page newsletters, $10. *Parent Express: For You and*
Your Toddler. 12 booklets, $4. ANR Publications, University of
California, 6701 San Pablo Avenue, Oakland, CA. 510.642.2431.
<anrcatalog.ucdavis.edu>
Wonderful series of newsletters for parents. The first set starts two months
before delivery and continues monthly through the first year of the child's
life. Second set with twelve letters covers second and third years. Good

resource for teen parents. Beautiful photos, easy reading.

Pollock, Sudie. ***Will the Dollars Stretch? Teen Parents Living on Their Own.*** 2001. 112 pp. $7.95. Teacher's Guide, $2.50. Morning Glory.
Five short stories about teen parents moving out on their own. As students read, they will get the feel of poverty as experienced by many teen parents — as they write checks and balance checkbooks of young parents involved.

_____. ***Moving On: Finding Information You Need for Living on Your Own.*** 2001. 48 pp. $4.95. 25/$75. Morning Glory Press.
Fill-in guide to help young persons find information about their community, information needed for living away from parents.

Porter, Connie. ***Imani All Mine.*** 1999. 218 pp. $12.95. Houghton Miflin.
Wonderful novel about a black teen mom in the ghetto where poverty, racism, and danger are constant realities.

Reynolds, Marilyn. **True-to-Life Series from Hamilton High:** *No More Sad Goodbyes, Shut Up!, Baby Help. Beyond Dreams. But What About Me? Detour for Emmy. Telling. Too Soon for Jeff, Love Rules, If You Loved Me.* 1993-2008. 160-256 pp. $8.95-$9.95. Morning Glory Press.
Wonderfully gripping stories about situations faced by teens. Start with **Detour for Emmy,** *award-winning novel about a 15-year-old mother. Students who read one of Reynolds' novels usually ask for more. Topics cover partner abuse, acquaintance rape, reluctant teen father, sexual molestation, racism, fatal accident, abstinence, homophobia, school failure.*

Sears, Martha and William. ***The Breastfeeding Book: Everything You Need to Know About Nursing Your Child from Birth Through Weaning.*** 2000. 272 pp. $14.99. Little, Brown.
Discusses, among other topics, the practical challenges of breastfeeding that confront many women who work away from home.

Seward, Angela. Illustrated by Donna Ferreiro. ***Goodnight, Daddy.*** 2001. 48 pp. Paper, $7.95; hardcover, $14.95. Morning Glory Press.
Beautiful full-color picture book shows Phoebe's excitement because of her father's visit today. She is devastated when he calls to say, "Something has come up." Book illustrates the importance of father in the life of his child.

Silberg, Jackie. ***Games to Play with Babies.*** 2001. 256 pp. $14.95. ***Games to Play with Toddlers.*** 2002. 256 pp. $14.95. Gryphon House.
Activities and games that don't require a lot of props.

Sweeney, Joyce. ***Waiting for June.*** 2006. 145 pp. $5.99. Marshall Cavendish.
Fantasy and realism are beautifully blended in this story of a teenage poet who becomes pregnant.

Walsh, David. *Why Do They Act That Way? Survival Guide to the Adolescent Brain for You and Your Teen.* 2005. 288 pp. $13.95. Free Press.
Explains changes in teens' brains and shows parents and others how to use this information to understand and communicate with teens.

Wiggins, Pamela K. *Why Should I Nurse My Baby?* 1998. 58 pp. $5.95. Noodle Soup, 4614 Prospect Avenue, #328, Cleveland, OH 44103. 216.881.5151.
Easy-to-read, yet thorough discussion of breastfeeding. Question and answer format. Also ask about the Babies First pamphlets, same source.

Williams-Wheeler, Dorrie. *The Unplanned Pregnancy Book for Teens & College Students.* 2004. 136 pp. $10.95. Sparkledoll Productions.
Step-by-step guide to the stages of pregnancy, assistance programs, childcare options, and expectations during prenatal care, breastfeeding, etc.

Wolff, Virginia E. *Make Lemonade.* 2006. 208 pp. $6.95. Henry Holt. *True Believer.* 2002. 272 pp. $8.99. Simon Pulse.
Wonderful novels about a teenager living in a Project and a young mom who becomes her friend.

Websites

All sites begin with www.

aap.org – American Academy of Pediatrics. Provides reliable information on many topics regarding child health and development.

acog.org – American College of Obstetricians and Gynecologists. Information about pregnancy and breastfeeding.

ada.org – American Dental Association. Good for information on nutrition, health, and dental health.

americandieteticassociation.org – Information on current dietary recommendations, gestational diabetes, fat and sodium recommendations. Also has site **eatright.org** for standards on child care nutrition.

arbys.com – Nutrition information on foods served here.

dairyqueen.com – Nutrition information on foods served at this chain.

usda.gov – **U.S. Department of Agriculture.** Wealth of information including **MyPyramid** for all ages.

futureofchildren.org – **Packard Foundation** site has timely publication regarding current research on many topics around children.

kfc.com – Information on dietary values of food served here.

lungoregon.org/tobacco/secondhand.html – Discussion of risks of inhaling second-hand smoke.

mcdonalds.com/app_controller.nutrition.Index1.html – Complete nutrition information on all foods served at McDonald's restaurants.

mypyramid.gov – U.S. Department of Agriculture. Put in your age, sex, and activity level, and you'll get a chart showing the foods *you* need. Do the same for your child 2 years or older.

nlm.nih.gov/medlineplus – National Institutes of Health site for reliable source of dietary information.

nrc.uchsc.edu – National Resource Center for Health and Safety in Child Care and Early Education.

DVDs — Sources, Representative Titles
(Contact distributors for current listings.)

Discipline from Birth to Three. Four DVDs, **Infants and Discipline — Meeting Baby's Needs, He's Crawling — Help!** (6-12 months), **She's into Everything!** (1-2 years), and **Your Busy Runabout** (2-3 years). 2001. 15 min. each. $195 set, $69.95 each. Morning Glory Press, 6595 San Haroldo Way, Buena Park, CA 90620. 888.612.8254.
Wonderful videos over book of same title. Shows teens talking to teens, sharing techniques for loving care. Teaching guide includes discussion questions, writing and research assignments, and quiz.

Healthy Steps for Teen Parents. Three DVDs, **"Prenatal Care," "Labor and Birth,"** and **"Postpartum."** 2001. 25 min. each. $195 each; 3/$499.95. Available in Spanish. Injoy Videos.
Series for teens features an all-teen cast. Teens will identify with real life footage as they meet a diverse group of peers who are successful teen parents. For example, in "Labor and Birth," viewers follow Marquita, a single 15-year-old mom, and 19-year-old Samantha and her supportive boyfriend. One chooses unmedicated childbirth, the other epidural pain relief.

Healthy Touch: Infant Massage for Teenage Parents. 40 min. $79.95. Injoy Videos.
Focusing on touch, the simple massage strokes are easy for teen parents to learn and incorporate into their daily contact with their babies. Introduction is for the teacher, but the rest of the film is designed for young parents, and is excellent.

Life Skills for Teen Parents. 2007. Two volume set, $349.95. 35 min. ea. Injoy Videos.
Realistic, down-to-earth series gives teens concrete suggestions for moving forward in their lives.

Project Future: Your Pregnancy, Your Plan. Giving Birth to Your Baby. Your New Baby, Your New Life. 42 to 56 min. each. 1991. One video, $99; 3 videos, $295. Vida Health Communications, 6 Bigelow Street, Cambridge, MA 02139. 617.864.4334.
Provide comprehensive help for pregnant and parenting teens. Each is divided into two parts, each of which can be used separately. Excellent videos, respectful to teen parents, informative, and entertaining. Offer emotional support as well as teaching basic parenting skills.

Reading with Babies. Directed by Susan Straub. 2006. $25.00. The Read to Me Program, Inc. POB 730 Planetarium Station, New York, NY 10024-0539. **<www.readtomeprogram.org>**
Wonderful video that shows babies 0-24 months 'reading' books with their parent(s) according to their developmental capacities. Realistic, playful portrayal of babies interacting with books.

Teen Breastfeeding: The Natural Choice. 20 min. **Teen Breastfeeding: Starting Out Right.** 35 min. Both for $139.95. Injoy Videos.
Wonderful videos. Part 1 provides reasons to breastfeed, and Part 2 tells how. Several teen moms star. A lactation specialist shows a young mom still in the hospital how to get her baby latched on to her breast. It's a fast moving and colorful series. I wish I had had it when I was breastfeeding our five kids.

Too Soon for Jeff. 1996. 40 min. $89.95. Films for the Humanities and Sciences, P.O. Box 2053, Princeton, NJ 08543. 800.257.5126.
ABC After-School TV Special was based on the award-winning novel by Marilyn Reynolds. Starring Freddie Prinze, Jr., it's an excellent adaptation of the novel about a reluctant teen father.

Voices: The Reality of Early Childbirth. 1998. 20 min. 89.95. Injoy Video.
Shows by example how teen parents can be good parents. Young parents, teens who are fully committed to their children, share their hopes and dreams, triumphs and frustrations.

Your Baby's First Year. 2001. Four DVDs. **Nurturing Your Newborn, She's Much More Active** (4-8 months), **Leaving Baby Stage Behind, Keeping Baby Healthy.** $195 set; $69.95 each. Morning Glory Press.
Teens talking to teens, sharing techniques for loving care. Based on book, with same title. Includes teacher's guide with questions, projects, quiz.

Index

Adoption, 25, 27, 57
Birth plan, 26
Brain development, 11, 49, 57
Breastfeeding, 26, 27, 130-133
Case studies, 151
Child reports, 59, 61, 121
Classroom lesson plans, 28,
    31-32, 61-63, 86-88, 89-91,
    112-113, 137-139, 168-170
Creativity in discipline, 166-167
Development, adolescent, 16
Discipline, 107, 158-181
Discussion quides, 39-41, 47,
    69-70, 75, 78-79, 96, 101,119,
    125, 146, 156, 175
Energy/discipline relationship,
    166
Environment and discipline, 164
Fast food, 127, 129, 137-156
Fetal development, 24
Fiction, 85-86

GRADS, 20
Grandparents, 10, 162-163, 164
Group leader, planning, 18, 32-
    33, 50, 63, 65, 86, 89, 91-92,
    113, 139, 170
Guidelines, teaching, 21
Health check-up, 43
Home visits, 18-21, 34, 50, 65,
    92, 113, 140 170-171
Independent study assignments,
    38, 68, 95, 118, 144, 145,
    174
Independent study, 18, 32, 55-56,
    110
Individualized study guide,
    postpartum, 53-54
Job skills, 100
Journal, 51, 56, 57
Learning activities, descriptions
    of, 36-38, 48-79, 94-95,
    115-118, 142-145, 173-174

Nutrition, 126-157

Nutrition facts, 148

Obesity, 140

Patience, in discipline, 165-166

Portions vs. servings, 130

Postpartum homestay, 50-57, 131

Prenatal health, 22-47

Prepared childbirth, 26

Pretest, nutrition, 128

Puzzles, 42, 71, 97, 120, 150, 152

Quizzes, 44-45, 76, 87, 124, 155

Rap session, 109

Read to Me Program, 83

Reader theater, 29-30, 72, 73-74, 153, 157

Reading Is Fundamental (RIF), 82-83

Reading, importance of, 80-92, 123

Realities, of teen parents, 162-163

Recipes, 154

Respect, in discipline, 159-161

Self-esteem, 160, 165

Shopping for food, 135

Solid food, introduction of, 133-134

Spanking, 107, 172-178

Speakers, outside, 28

Spoiling baby, impossibility of, 27, 29-30, 162, 163-164

Statistics, reading, 84

Statistics, teen parents, 16

Straub, Susan, 83

Teaching standards, 20

Teaching to the present, 16-17

Teen dads, 102-125

Teen dads, resources for, 110-111

Teed dads, rights, 105

Trust/discipline relationship, 167-168

Vegetarianism, 136-137

Walsh, David, Ph.D., 11-12

Morning Glory Press
6595 San Haroldo Way, Buena Park, CA 90620
714.828.1998; 888.612.8254   Fax 1.888.327.4362
email info@morningglorypress.com   www.morningglorypress.com

	Price	Total
__ **Complete *Teens Parenting* Curriculum**	$1236.00	_____

One each — Six *Comprehensive Curriculum Notebooks*
plus 11 books, 7 workbooks, 8 videos/DVDs, 5 games
(as listed below)
Buy text and workbook for each student. — Quantity discounts.

__ *The P.A.R.E.N.T. Approach*	12.95	_____
__ *ROAD to Fatherhood*	14.95	_____

Resources for Teen Parents:

__ *Mommy, I'm Hungry!* Quality paper	12.95	_____
__ *Mommy, I'm Hungry!* Hardcover	18.95	_____
__ *Mommy, I'm Hungry! Curriculum Notebook*	125.00	
__ *Your Pregnancy and Newborn Journey*	12.95	_____
__ **Easier Reading Edition (GL2)**	12.95	_____
__ *Tu embarazo y el nacimiento de tu bebé*	12.95	_____
__ *PNJ Curriculum Notebook*	125.00	
__ **PNJ Board Game**	34.95	_____
__ **Pregnancy Two-in-One Bingo**	24.95	_____
__ *Nurturing Your Newborn*	7.95	_____
__ **Easier Reading Edition (GL2)**	7.95	_____
__ *Crianza del recién nacido*	7.95	
__ *Your Baby's First Year*	12.95	_____
__ **Easier Reading Edition (GL2)**	12.95	_____
__ *El primer año del bebé*	12.95	_____
__ *NN/BFY Comprehensive Curriculum Notebook*	125.00	_____
__ **Four DVDs – Baby's First Year Series**	195.00	_____
__ **Baby's First Year Board Game**	34.95	_____
__ *Discipline from Birth to Three*	12.95	_____
__ **Easier Reading Edition (GL2)**	12.95	_____
__ *La disciplina hasta los tres años*	12.95	
__ *Discipline from Birth to Three Curriculum Notebook*	125.00	_____
__ **Four DVDs – Discipline from Birth to Three Series**	195.00	_____
__ **Discipline from Birth to Three Board Game**	34.95	_____
__ *The Challenge of Toddlers*	12.95	_____
__ *El reto de los párvulos*	12.95	
__ *CT Curriculum Notebook*	125.00	_____
__ **Challenge of Toddlers Board Game**	34.95	_____
SUBTOTAL (Carry over to top of next page.)		_____

SUBTOTAL FROM PREVIOUS PAGE _____

__ *Teen Dads: Rights, Responsibilities and Joys*	12.95	_____
__ *Teen Dads Curriculum Notebook*	125.00	_____
__ *The Softer Side of Hip-Hop*	9.95	_____
__ *Read to Me! I Will Listen* (10/$25; 25/$50; 100/$150)	2.95	_____

More Resources for Teen Parents

Following books are NOT included in Complete *Teens Parenting* Curriculu

__ *Moving On*	4.95	_____
__ *Will the Dollars Stretch?*	7.95	_____
__ *Breaking Free from Partner Abuse*	8.95	_____
__ *Dreams to Reality: Help for Young Moms*	14.95	_____
__ *Do I Have a Daddy?* Hardcover	14.95	_____
__ *Goodnight, Daddy* Hardcover	14.95	_____
__ *Did My First Mother Love Me?* Hardcover	12.95	_____
__ *Pregnant? Adoption Is an Option*	12.95	_____
__ *Surviving Teen Pregnancy*	12.95	
__ *Safer Sex: The New Morality*	14.95	_____
__ *Teen Moms: The Pain and the Promise*	14.95	_____

Novels by Marilyn Reynolds:

__ *Shut Up!*	9.95	_____
__ *No More Sad Goodbyes*	9.95	
__ *Love Rules*	9.95	_____
__ *If You Loved Me*	8.95	_____
__ *Baby Help*	8.95	_____
__ *But What About Me?*	8.95	_____
__ *Too Soon for Jeff*	9.95	_____
__ *Detour for Emmy*	9.95	_____
__ *Telling*	8.95	_____
__ *Beyond Dreams*	8.95	_____

SUBTOTAL _____

Add postage: 10% of total—Min., $3.50; 20%, Canada _____

California residents add 7.75% sales tax _____

TOTAL _____

Ask about quantity discounts, teacher, student guides.

Prepayment requested. School/library purchase orders accepted.

NAME_____

PHONE _____ Purchase Order # _____

ADDRESS_____

_____